Marching to a Silent Tune

Enter the journey, though lost and unsure.

Enter the journey, God's peace will be yours.

And all who are thirsting be filled with God's grace....

Enter the journey, though dark is the way.

Enter the journey, do not be afraid,

for God's great compassion will give you new sight.

Enter the journey of light!

Mark Friedman and Janet Vogt

Dedication

With Love
For my Katie…and our tribe.
The adventure continues.

With Deep Respect
For my fellow resisters—military and civilian.
Especially those at the Fort Lewis "Bay of Pigs."

With Enduring Gratitude
For those who stood by me back in the day.
Especially Constance Tomon, Jim Forest,
Tom Cornell, and Charles Talbot.

In Memory of
Bill Gooding (KIA 19 August 1969),
the others on the Wall,
and all who suffered
before, during, and after the Vietnam War.
We never forget.

Marching to a Silent Tune

A Journey from We Shall to Hell No

GERALD R. GIOGLIO

MARCHING TO A SILENT TUNE
A Journey from We Shall to Hell No
Gerald R. Gioglio

Editing by Martin Foner and Gregory F. Augustine Pierce
Cover and text design and typesetting by Andrea Reider
Cover photo "Insignia" by Justin Killian, used with permission
Verses from "Enter the Journey" by Mark Friedman and Janet Vogt,
    used with permission

Published by ACTA Publications, (800) 397-2282, www.actapublications.com

Grateful acknowledgement for permission to reprint earlier published
versions of "Induction Station" (aka "Maggot Days") and "Wheels on the
Bus," which appeared in the Fall 2017 and the Spring 2018 issues of *The
Veteran*, the newspaper of the Vietnam Veterans Against the War

The stories and quotations in this book are true, although some of the
details may have been influenced by the author's memory of the events
described. A few names and details in this book have been intentionally
changed to honor the privacy or feelings of people involved.

Library of Congress Catalog number: 2022941323
ISBN: 978-0-87946-701-2
Printed in the United States of America by Total Printing Systems
Year 30 29 28 27 26 25 24 23
Printing 10 9 8 7 6 5 4 3 2
Text printed on 30% post-consumer recycled paper

Contents

Introduction

——•——

Start by doing what's necessary;
then do what's possible;
and suddenly you are doing the impossible.

Francis of Assisi

"So, what'd you do in the war, dad?" Today it could just as easily be, "So, what'd you do in the war, mom?" It is a question many veterans, from too many different generations and wars, tend to dance around, if we address it at all.

How often we hear something like, "My father, mother, aunt, uncle, brother, sister, wife, husband, son, daughter, cousin, friend never talks about the war." Here's why: Talking about war is extremely personal. For many veterans, war is a question about valor, patriotism, identity itself—often traumatic, nightmarish, best to be forgotten. For others, war is just something that happened, best not to be revisited. Asking someone what they did in the war comes with the unstated but assumed expectation of stories of courage and bravery under unimaginable conditions. Or perhaps it assumes a story of perseverance, of doing one's duty, of keeping one's head down, of volunteering (or never doing so).

But what we tend to fail to anticipate is that many veterans, especially men and women from the Vietnam War era, also have extraordinary *peace stories* to share, which are all too often dismissed as neither courageous nor brave. In both cases—war stories or peace stories—the question of what one did "during the war" looms large.

These peace stories often tell the tale of patriotic in-service resistance, of a refusal to be re-socialized after the war, of rejecting something—not just military life but a certain outlook on life itself. They are stories of rejecting the nature of war, its legality, its morality; of refusing orders, legal or illegal; of being court-martialed or perhaps going to prison for one's beliefs. For many of us, it is something that went beyond the personal and morphed into collective action—perhaps quiet or active resistance, getting involved in the GI-Civilian movement for peace, or other in-service antiwar activities.

These peace stories are sometimes about protest or confrontation; or about individual or collective resistance or compromise; or about something happening before being shipped to a combat zone, or sometimes after fighting a war.

———•———

This book tells my story of in-service resistance to the war in Vietnam that began in my childhood days, when the subtle seeds of social justice were planted, including the spiritual, social, and cultural influences that led me to this witness. It is written as a personal narrative, a memoir, because that is what it is. Still, to tell the tale accurately, it is important for me to incorporate the predominant social and cultural realities of the time. While my peace story occurred fifty years ago, it contains strong memories of things I have never forgotten. The details here are backed up by military and civil intelligence files collected at that time.

In weaving this account together, my mind often turns to those who are now in the military; those convinced they are doing their duty by being part of today's military operations from the Middle East to Ukraine to who knows where next. I especially think of those who find themselves in a position where, for reasons of conscience, they can no longer participate in the military or in war-making. I also assume the military draft—this time for both women and men—that my generation fought so hard to eliminate, may someday be brought back. So, in large measure, my thinking in this book must consider the present and future generations who will have to confront the reality of war and their participation in it.

If there are errors of omission here, they are solely mine. I strive to adhere to the "nonfiction contract" of telling it like it was, and any shortcomings were not meant to mislead. I do know memory can play tricks. Often, there is selective forgetting and a tendency to cherry-pick recollections. There is also an inclination to either simplify or excessively explain things by painting word-pictures in much sharper relief than they deserve. I accept that; then again, I know what I know, and as you will see I have many documents to rely on. Some things you can never forget; nor should they be forgotten. Nor should they go untold, even if they relate a twenty-year old's story written with a seventy-year-old's memory.

What appears here is a humble attempt to get it all down— from my early personal and religious training to the experiences, frustrations, doubts, fears, and compromises involved when attempting to stand up for my beliefs.

———•———

This narrative is presented in four parts:

- Part I speaks to my growing up Catholic and its emphasis on social justice, especially as it related to the Civil Rights Movement. We will consider the tumultuous 1960s and the thinking and behavior of many of us growing up at the time. Included are certain events and experiences that impacted my thinking, like being attracted to underdogs and those clamoring for racial equality during a time that was often ethnically and racially insensitive, indeed prejudiced, a time not that different from today. The experience of being mentored by a socially conscious priest during my teenage years is also detailed. Included are short vignettes of his efforts to educate my friends and I on civil liberties issues and to connect us to civil rights organizations. There is also a discussion of my early thoughts and feelings during interactions with the Selective Service System.
- Part II details my initial introduction to Basic Training and my attempts to be recognized as someone who was opposed to the war. There are also discussions about the military environment, protocols, and discipline. Finally, there is an overview of weapons handling, especially experiences on the firing line and during bayonet training.
- Part III focuses on military life and instruction during Advanced Infantry Training at Fort Polk, Louisiana.

Included are discussions of light-arms weaponry and techniques used by the infantry in Southeast Asia. Attention is given to the developing GI antiwar effort, with a look at subtle incidents of defiance correlating with the growing GI opposition to the war. Most importantly, I trace the systematic crystallization of antiwar beliefs developed during training, including the thoughts, doubts, fears, and methods used to distance ourselves from militarism and find some inner peace. There is a related discussion of my running afoul of the system and experiencing epiphanies that affected my thinking.

- Part IV presents a personal account of in-service war resistance at Fort Lewis, Washington, with emphasis on the local GI-civilian antiwar movement. It includes an overview of a wonderful fellowship I developed with a group of other war resisters, all of them waiting for discharge or court-martial for refusing to ship to Vietnam. There is also a look at everyday military assignments that led to formal and informal ways of helping other GIs who were questioning the war or otherwise needed assistance with hardship or other issues. Besides the focus on fighting back, there is a look at the stress and emotions generated by uncertainty over our cases and by watching—one by one—members of our fellowship pay the price for their resistance.

Absent from this entire narrative are the many and varied personal and familial experiences of that historical time. That is, the struggle to grow up, the trials of being a young-adult husband, the litany of youthful missteps and mistakes, and the sins of my youth.

To be clear, I do not seek recognition for any contribution I made in those days. This was a group effort. For many of us, this resistance to war simply needed to be done.

We had to believe the Constitution meant something. We had to end the killing; we had to end the military draft; we had to end the war.

My goal here is threefold:

- To provide a witness, a guide perhaps, for those who may someday find themselves caught up in a similar situation.
- To educate others about the reality of military training and what happens to those who go through it even if they end up with no combat experience.
- To underscore the historical importance of the in-service resistance to the Vietnam War.

With this book I seek to present something honoring the witness of those patriots who traveled a similar road to mine, while still respecting those warriors who believed in and fought in Vietnam and other conflicts. Despite our differences, we all were—and will always be—in this together.

Gerald R. Gioglio
May 7, 2022
47th Anniversary of the End of the Vietnam War

PART I

———▶ ● ◀———

We Shall!

Today, as yesterday, I am just a guy; once an average kid of my time, born into a working-class family of Sicilian and German heritage and raised very, *very* Catholic. I took that faith tradition seriously. As a youth, I attended twelve years of Catholic schooling and did well in religion classes. I learned much about both the liturgy and negative behaviors. I also tuned in to messages about doing "the next right thing" like raising money for and lifting up the poor, supporting civil liberties, and in all cases following my conscience.

But looking back, I realize trying to do good did not necessarily mean it was going to be easy or that all my actions would be appreciated. Early on, I did not fully comprehend I should expect to be persecuted for the good I believed I was trying to achieve. Beyond not completely internalizing this message, I do know I was given a solid foundation in family, church, and school that would prove to guide my many future actions.

Thus, if there is a word of caution in this work it is this: When you stand up to power remember—like a prophet crying out in the desert—you can expect sand will be kicked in your face. Or, as we Catholics might say: Remember to pick up your cross. A naïve kid, I did not expect either sand or the need to carry a heavy burden for following my conscience. I had yet to understand the oft-repeated warning, "No good deed goes unpunished." I did not fully understand my entire generation had to grow up very quickly, accept historical realities, wipe the sand from our faces, and be prepared to suffer—insults, threats, legalities, incarceration…and our own fears. Thank God I was not alone in this. We were legion.

Sometimes I wonder why I internalized Catholic Social Teaching that, as I recall, was not even called that back then; but I did. In some small way, what occurred in the run-up to and experience of my military days was being guided, perhaps even haunted, by what I learned as a boy. I'm not going to deny it. It can't be denied. It can't be ignored. It just was not immediately recognized nor consistently applied during a time when counterculture and secularism beckoned. Something approaching sacredness seems out of reach and perhaps takes a lifetime to discover, let alone apply.

I have told some resistance stories before from the perspectives of others who lived them. In the book, *Days of Decision: An Oral History of Conscientious Objectors in the Military during the Vietnam War*, I presented the experiences of twenty-four in-service war objectors. These include those who came into the military as non-combatant conscientious objectors, and those who applied for it after some experience of military life. These were varied stories of upbringing, training, military experience, and ultimately joining the resistance, perhaps by seeking discharge or going to prison.

When I wrote *Days of Decision,* I designed it in a way that did not take me too far from my training as a sociologist. Full disclosure: I do not want to overstate that academic title, for although I very nearly completed a PhD in Sociology, I never earned the degree. Still, I spent a career doing research and evaluation for the State of New Jersey and often taught Sociology classes part-time at various colleges. I loved it all.

As I told the stories in *Days of Decision,* I was thinking and writing like a sociologist, not as a participant. I decided to leave my own full story out. I thought the stories of those I interviewed should stand alone. I still believe this was the correct decision. But some readers wished I had also included my complete story. With this book I am addressing this criticism and to humbly, yet proudly, responding to the question I posed at the beginning of the Introduction: What I did in the Vietnam War.

Let's be clear. Like most of us at the time, I was just a child-man who was swept up into a phenomenally disruptive and murderous war being waged in our names. Not a saint, not yet much of a sinner, but a guy out of my league; someone with something inside screaming what the government was doing was very wrong. This was not something I—or any of us— should be involved in, ever.

Although I was inexplicably attracted to them, I was not like some of the great heroes of the time: Daniel Berrigan or Thomas Merton, the writers, or Dorothy Day, the peace and anti-nuclear activist. Nor was I a leader like David Hartsough, a Christian activist who worked tirelessly to end the Vietnam War and spent a lifetime working to build a more peaceful world. I was not as committed as those in the Fellowship of Reconciliation, the War Resisters League, or so many other organizations promoting an end to war. That said, I did become a lifer in the peace movement, just one of many troops involved in countless peace and social justice issues over the years. I was just not like the brave souls who purposely and actively dedicated their entire lives to working for peace and justice. I was none of these. I was just a guy who struggled with notions of right and wrong, Christian nonviolence, patriotism, and masculinity. Just one among a great mass of concerned citizens who took a stand and tried to end militarism and endless war.

First

———•———

Good Seeds

Let me fix my feet on that step
where as a boy I was placed by my parents
until clear truth is found.
But where may it be sought?

Augustine of Hippo

October 4, 1955, was the feast of Saint Francis of Assisi. Who knew, then or now? Certainly not me, the eight-year-old boy who flew home after school to turn on the TV to catch the last couple innings of Game 7 of the World Series between the Yankees and my beloved Brooklyn Dodgers.

Undoubtedly some of the 62,465 who crowded Yankee Stadium that day and the millions of fans who were glued to radios and TV screens were aware of the feast day. No doubt some fans went to Mass that morning to pray to the "Poor Man of Assisi" for the success of their favorite team.

I am sure all the nuns at our school were aware it was the feast of the most popular saint in the Catholic Church, but I'm betting the feast day was trumped by the game; indeed, our classroom Sister had it on the radio.

As a lifelong baseball fan, it is hard for me to understate the enormity of this event for fans in the New York area and across the nation. The Dodgers and Yankees were cross-town rivals, and this was the fifth World Series they played together over a nine-year period. The Yanks always won, prompting the rally cry, "Wait'll next year" from every hopeful fan of "dem bums." The Brooklyn Dodgers were perennial underdogs, the talented, loveable losers who all too often reached the top rung of the ladder only to fall back down, time and again. Loved by masses of metropolitan New Yorkers, some Dodger fans were known to pray the Rosary for the team, and notably for Gil Hodges when he suffered through a terrible batting slump. That this really happened was confirmed through many hot-stove chinwags with elderly baseball fans over the years.

For me, there was another reason to love those Dodgers: Jackie Robinson. In 1947, the Dodgers broke baseball's color barrier, becoming the first team to integrate the sport. Robinson had a rough time of it. It is well known that as the first African American major leaguer he had to win over teammates, fans, and players from other teams, many of whom were cruel and abusive. My child's eyes watched Robinson closely. He was, in baseball terms, a *gamer*, that is, he came to play. He came to play hard; he could hit, he could field, and—Lord, have mercy—Jackie could run. He did all this while constantly under attack; and yet, he played through it. He held his head high while demonstrating a quiet dignity that amazed and confused young fans like me who desperately wanted him to succeed.

What the Dodgers did for Robinson, and ultimately for African Americans, and the country, was right and just. Virtually every kid in my multi-ethnic, working-class neighborhood agreed; sadly, we could not say the same for the adults in our lives. Prejudice and outright racism ran deep and, as neighborhoods slowly became more diverse, our communities soon witnessed the onset of white flight draining cities large and small of working and middle-class white families.

But on this day, prejudice took a back seat to beating those Yanks. Unfortunately, the great Robinson who contributed so much to the team's success had to sit out the game with a strained Achilles tendon.

———•———

Doris Kearns Goodwin, in her wonderful memoir, *Wait Till Next Year,* details that Dodger season and the drama of Game 7 of the 1955 baseball classic. No one could write it better. Reading it some fifty years later transported me back to the very day, one so indelibly imprinted in my mind and psyche. Picture this: the bottom of the ninth inning…starting pitcher Johnny Podres still on the mound…Dodgers ahead 2-0…then suddenly two outs…a ground ball to shortstop...Reese to Hodges at first. Game over! Dodgers win!

And incredibly, like so many other Dodger fans everywhere, there I was jumping up and down…laughing and crying…running around in circles. A pure, simple gift of joy that somehow led me, at age eight, to begin to intuit that God loves us and wants us to be happy.

Looking back on those times, it is now clear several other insights were seeded in me that day: underdogs and the oppressed can prevail; prejudice and racism can be overcome; the dignified and heroic example can be emulated; and through cooperation, teamwork, persistence, and prayer we can stand up for our beliefs, overcome failure, and achieve redemption.

I have heard it said and have come to accept that there are no coincidences; things happen for a reason. That is what happened on this glorious day of pure joy, this Feast of Francis of Assisi. When I revisit this day, I accept that baseball somehow marked the clumsy emergence of a bumpy spiritual path—one that, unbeknownst to me, became entwined with Francis' message of peace, social justice, and care for creation. For me, October 4, 1955, marked not only the seeding of a social consciousness but the beginning of some sort of mystical brotherhood with the saint. Two things are certain: 1) as the years went on, the social justice teachings of the Catholic Church resonated with me more and more, and 2) the call of the Poor Man of Assisi emerged from time to time along my journey.

Second

—•—

The 'Hood

Wisdom grows from disillusionment.

Rev. Hans Urs von Balthasar

New Brunswick, New Jersey, aka the "Hub City," got its nickname for being a hub for travelers and traders between New York and Philadelphia. Early on this included the Delaware and Raritan Canal and Kings Highway, eventually leading to a rail stop that became part of the Northeast Corridor, and easy access to major highways including the New Jersey Turnpike.

In the 1950s and 1960s, our city of about 40,000 boasted a thriving downtown with three movie theatres, two supermarkets, both mom-and-pop and big-name stores like Sears and Woolworths. Downtown was open late on Thursdays and was a mob-scene on Saturdays. The streets were often filled with cars and the sidewalks packed with shoppers and pedestrians. On Sunday, most shops downtown were closed as required by the so called "Blue Laws" of the time, when businesses closed for the Christian Sabbath.

Redmond Street between Throop and Remsen Avenues was a multi-ethnic residential block with small family businesses on three corners. There were lots of kids in our essentially working-class neighborhood; after all, it was the post-World War II "baby boom." GIs from WWII and the Korean War returned, found spouses, and increased and multiplied. In my town, the kids filled the classrooms and the streets, the fathers the workplace and the bars, and the mothers the church and the homes. According to the adults, people were making money and there were plenty of jobs in factories, construction, and retail. There was great excitement about the federal government building an Interstate Highway system to improve travel and commerce all over the nation.

Our street was multi-ethnic, like a few other slowly changing neighborhoods in town. It featured a working-class African-American family and a Chinese family who ran a laundry and lived just around the corner on Throop Avenue. There was a neighborhood bar owned by a Lebanese immigrant family, and an Italian father-daughter team ran a grocery store on the first floor, had a residence on the second, and operated a small winery in the basement. We also had a Jewish family who owned two lots in the middle of the block and ran a small junk yard recycling metal. We also had a dirt-poor, multi-generational Irish family led by an inebriated and ornery old sod we kids called "Lester the Drunk." There were two ancient spinster sisters in a ramshackle house in need of both paint and repairs that we were sure was haunted and dared not approach.

When the schools emptied out, the street swarmed with children of multiple ethnicities. True, we were mostly white, but still, something of a "Rainbow Coalition" before anybody ever heard of Jesse Jackson. It was a chaotic cacophony of childhood spirit; a force of nature—shouting, laughing, arguing—kids playing stickball, football, dodge-ball, jump rope, hide and seek; roller skating in summer, sledding in winter…often grabbing onto car bumpers for the ride uphill when the street was snow covered.

This block belonged to *us*. Adults, especially those in cars who did not live on the block, were less than welcome. Screams of "Car, Car, C-A-R" was the warning to stop the games, step toward the curb, and let the interlopers pass. The more intense the game, the more intolerant of interruptions we kids tended to be. We verbally discouraged intruders from driving through with cat-calls such as, "Hey, you blind? We got a game going here." Or, "Hey, Brooklyn Cowboy, slow down! Where'd you get your license, Sears and Roebuck?"

The street belonged to us—*all of us,* white, black, brown, yellow; Catholic, Protestant, Jewish, Buddhist; boys and girls. We laughed together, we cried together, we fussed mightily; but rarely did we come to blows. Occasionally, one of us launched an errant ball through somebody's window. Remarkably, given the tight confines of our city street and the amount of stickball being played, this was quite rare; but when it did happen, we pooled our small change and accepted donations from parents to pay for the repairs.

—•—

Race and ethnicity were huge factors for the adults, most of whom felt threatened by the diversity. Sadly, the solidarity and equality we felt among ourselves did not extend to many of the adults in our lives, nor did we find it in most of our homes. It seemed all the adults in our neighborhood held some kind of prejudice against one group or another, often against more than one; African Americans and Jews particularly got most of the abuse.

Adults taught their kids an astonishing number of slurs to refer to various ethnic groups. So established and common was this practice, most kids just accepted these references as harmless nicknames. You might be known as a Mic, Wop, Chink, Spic, Kraut. We thought it was all just part of the vernacular. So, I was a Wop (meaning "<u>Wi</u>th<u>o</u>ut <u>P</u>apers"—a label originally affixed to the lapel of Italian immigrants who arrived without documents). I didn't know that at the time, but I was cool with the acronym. As far as I was concerned, I was thoroughly American and totally divorced from the European culture of my ancestors.

As an Italian kid my favorite handle was "Spaghetti Bender." It seemed there was something noble and delicious in this particular moniker. If you can suspend your righteous indignation today and step back, you just might be able to understand why that moniker appealed to me.

- *Spaghetti*: a pasta in the Italian meaning "little strings," tasty little strings I might add.
- *Bender*: one who twirls "little strings" with a fork and spoon.
- *Spaghetti Bender*: One who bends and twirls tasty little strings smothered in tomato gravy. Whoa, Momma Mia!

Suddenly, I am liking this five-syllable epithet, "Spaghetti Bender" a whole lot more than the blunt, monosyllabic "Wop." Let me quote a wise, anonymous old sage who once famously said, "Call me what you want, just don't call me late for dinner." Back then, that's *exactly* what I was talkin' about.

———•———

Even we kids, however, did notice the adults saved their worst invectives for African Americans and Jews. These were generally preceded by certain words kids were not supposed to hear or repeat. On one hand, the adults did not mind kids using slurs to refer to various ethnics; but they came down hard on us when it came to certain words and specific situations.

My first inclination ethnic insults were rude and intrinsically wrong came one day when I was hurrying out the door to play. I came running down the stairs making a beeline for the front door and screamed out to my mother, "I'm going to the Chink's." I was stopped dead in my tracks with a "Hold on young man!" It was just here I encountered my first feelings of cognitive dissonance as mother patiently, yet forcefully, instructed me to never use the word *Chink* again when referring to our Chinese neighbors. She was insistent such name calling was rude, insulting, and hurtful. I'm standing there in total disbelief, like, "What?" In the world of men and boys such language was ubiquitous and expected. Confused, I accepted what this gentle and sensitive woman said. And I began to think about it, as the first uncertain rays of sensitivity began to break through.

(Fifty-odd years later, my twelve-year-old grandson, so steeped in messages of equality between races and genders, once referred to one of his friends as a "faggot." His mother *and* his grandmother jumped all over him as the mystified child experienced his own first encounter with an ugly truth. "All the boys say that," he declared in his defense. And, of course, he was being truthful. I sat there experiencing what the great baseball player and unlikely sage Yogi Berra referred to as "déjà vu all over again." My grandson and I chatted about it later, leaving me convinced this is one reason God made grandfathers.)

I was blessed with two of the kindest, gentlest parents a kid could have, but I came to discover they, too, held racial biases—more benign than most but nevertheless real, a product of their upbringing and their times. Those times included living in a city where, for decades, ethnics clustered in neighborhoods defined by heritage and religion. In Catholic sections of New Brunswick, for example, there were two Irish neighborhoods, also an Italian, a Hungarian, and a German neighborhood—each with their own Catholic churches and schools. In the 1860s, my maternal great-grandparents helped to build and administer the German church, St. John the Baptist, but my family attended the Irish church in our neighborhood.

Many Catholic white ethnics had experienced discrimination, especially in the early part of the twentieth century, especially the Irish and the Italians. My German-American mother told a tale from the 1920s when she decided to marry my Sicilian-American father. Apparently, one of her girlfriends said to her, "How can you go to bed with a Dago?" She got a kick out of relaying this tale many decades later, but it must have stung at the time. Quite simply, most people learn to be ethnocentric and closed; some learn to get over it, others don't.

Our parish, the Church of the Sacred Heart, was one of the earliest Catholic churches built in the city; its cornerstone read "1883." It was originally funded and constructed through the gifts and labor of the up-and-coming Irish American families in the area. The parish filled an entire city block, including the church building, a convent for the Sisters of Charity, a grotto honoring Mary, and the Sacred Heart Elementary School. The bas-relief over the front entrance of the school depicted Christ with some disciples welcoming a group of children. The inscription read, "Suffer the little children to come unto Me;" and we did. In droves.

During the week, we sat at the feet of the nuns learning about inequality and the plight of minorities in America. On Sunday, we listened to sermons promoting justice for all Americans, decrying segregated schools and drinking fountains, and describing the black people who were hung from trees in the cruel, hot oppression of the American South.

Beyond my little world defined by neighborhood and church, our town also featured a Jewish synagogue, several Protestant churches, and an assortment of store-front and other more elaborate African-American churches. I did not know if the Jews and the Protestants also clustered by neighborhood, but I did know that most African American people occupied the oldest and poorest neighborhoods of New Brunswick along the Raritan River. Indeed, I witnessed the complete destruction of these communities as the federal government provided urban renewal money to move the poor out of their rented (or sometimes even owned) one- and two-family homes and then warehouse them in segregated, high-rise projects.

———•———

My mother and father were the oldest parents on the block. My dad, born in 1901, was too young for World War I and too old to be called into World War II. A master plumber, he contributed to the war effort by working in the shipyards and doing volunteer civilian service work.

He was a little guy, 5'6" and maybe 140 pounds soaking wet, but a man's man, rugged due to the backbreaking nature of his trade. He liked to watch boxing, wrestling, Westerns; and he savored beer, Seagram's 7, and home-rolled cigarettes. Dad was not just older but, unlike most of the young married males in the neighborhood, he had not been directly touched by war; the difference was striking. We didn't know about Post-Traumatic Stress Disorder in the 1950s and 1960s; but looking back it is now obvious many veterans in my neighborhood were affected by PTSD.

Many of these younger guys drank too much and were mean to their wives and kids; you sometimes heard anguished shouts and arguments coming out of their homes. In the street, there were just some men you stayed away from. You did not try to joke around with or provoke these guys for fear of initiating a drunken rage. Other adults, however, were fair game for any number of childhood pranks.

Many of my friends admitted to being afraid of their dads. But they loved mine, and he loved kids; he was a Teddy Bear at heart, especially goofy after a shot and a beer. Too old and totally hopeless at sports and games, he always had a kind word and a laugh, trinkets, or candy to share with my friends.

In the privacy of our home, my parents presented a darker side when it came to race. My mother was appalled by things like Klan violence and the periodic lynching that continued to occur in the South. My father leaned toward a racial hierarchy, with white priority. They both believed in the separation of the races—"separate but equal"—before that term even entered the national discourse. Or, as they told me one time, "Jerry, it's best that people stay with their own." Still, years later I came to understand my parents were more benign than most; indeed, my dad was more like Archie Bunker than a Ku Klux Klanner. When he died, a total stranger came up to me and said, "Your father was the gentlest man I ever knew." He shook my hand and walked away. Those have been some tough shoes for me to fill right there.

———•———

Our forays off the block made us aware attitudes and behaviors were even worse beyond the narrow confines of our interracial neighborhood. For example, there was only one swimming pool in town, about a mile from our neighborhood. You could bike there, and kids who were members often did. It turns out the white owner refused to allow African Americans to use the pool. He got around this by setting it up as a privately-owned swim club, admitting only those he deemed eligible. Some people were happy about this and defended the owner's right to run his business as he pleased. This went on for years until the city hired its first African-American police officer, who demanded that he and his family be allowed to join the pool. I cannot recall if there was a court case or simply the threat of one. Whatever happened, rather than integrate the pool, the owner closed it and sold the property, turning it into an urban strip mall.

One evening over dinner my parents reprimanded me saying I had been seen downtown with one of my African-American friends. This, they advised, was not proper behavior because "people will talk." I'm not sure what admonitions or cautions other ethnic families gave to their offspring, but it did not matter. For the most part, I was fine with "Honor thy father and thy mother," but this—this—did not sit well with me or most of my friends. It simply made no sense and could not be justified.

Still, we mostly obeyed, although many of us continued to learn sometimes we had to stand up to tradition, custom, and authority. So, beyond the great divide separating adults from the kid world, we learned to respect our elders but also to go our own way to walk in the shoes of others before passing judgment. Sometimes, it was hard to juggle these two things.

For example, some of the women in our neighborhood would often ask one of us to run to the store. This was cool, because you usually got a tip for your trouble, keeping you in gum or soda for the day. Generally, one of the white kids was picked, but I think we naively just saw this as adults picking their favorites because of friendships with a family or whatever.

The gal who always chose me was a middle-aged lady who lived smack dab in the middle of our block, right in the vortex of all the noisy kid action you might imagine. Let's call her Mrs. Jones. She'd step out on the stoop, call me over, tell me what to get, and reward me with small change on my return. It worked for me.

The kids never dwelled much on why she lived alone or why she hardly ever came out of her house, but the adults knew. It turns out *her* husband, a taxi-driver, a few years before had driven himself out to Farrington Lake on the outskirts of town, pulled out a pistol, and blew his brains out. Back then I did not understand her loss and pain. One day, despite the admonition to respect one's elders, I stood up to her for dissing one of my African-American friends.

The kids slowly began to realize it was only the white kids on our block who were asked to run chores for the ladies; never the Chinese kids, never the black kids. One day, I was exhausted from playing and out of sorts. But when Mrs. Jones called me to go to the store, I yelled back at her, "Tony will do it." Every other

Tony I knew was of Italian descent, but this particular Tony was one of the African-American kids on the block … and my buddy.

Mrs. Jones got clearly flustered and called on another white kid to run her chores. Then, I lost it. The next thing I knew I was on the stoop and in her face criticizing her for what I perceived was her prejudicial behavior. I do not remember what was said, but I remember feeling justice had been served.

I guess I was not surprised when my saintly mother read me the riot act later that afternoon. Mrs. Jones had called and told her I'd been rude. I explained the situation and desperately tried to convince my mother that Mrs. Jones was prejudiced and I was just doing the right thing. I reminded her of what we were being taught at school and in the sermons about racial equality we listened to on Sunday. That got me nowhere. I got the standard "always respect your elders" speech and was ordered to march up to Mrs. Jones' house and apologize, "Right this very minute."

Oh, the humiliation. Oh, the feeling of betrayal. Not yet eleven years old, I'm standing there dumbfounded. How do I process this? What do you do with this when you see African Americans living beyond our block who, unlike Tony's family, were not working-class but poor? Poor people, with no job opportunities, walking everywhere or driving ramshackle cars, living in substandard housing, hoping the American dream was in reach but knowing they could never get out of their current nightmare. That somehow, sometime, this dream would be obtainable even for them, no, especially for them; these the descendants of slaves, who helped to build our nation. What do you do with this when you see prejudice on your own block—the dirty looks, the unkind words—worse, the indifference, as if to ignore their very presence was one way to wish them away? What do you do with this if you do not at least stand up for your friends?

I was offended and defensive and thought, *Ah, Mom, how about "La Familia? You know, sticking up for your kid—me? This kid, the one the good Sisters sometimes referred to as "a bold, brazen article." That kid who thought he was doing the right thing and was trying to make you proud?*

Well, there was nothing for it. I trudged up the street, rang the bell, took a deep breath, and reluctantly apologized for being rude. Mrs. Jones never asked me to go to the store for her again. That worked for me.

Yet this was the only time I was ever truly disappointed with my mother. And over time, I have realized she was motivated by compassion for Mrs. Jones' loss and situation; something a little kid could not understand. Slowly, I was also beginning to realize some things were just not fair and, if you really wanted to be a prophet crying out in the desert, you'd better be prepared for some sand to be kicked in your face.

Third

White Privilege

All human beings are…entitled to all the rights and freedoms set forth in this Declaration…such as race, colour, sex, language, religion, political or other opinion, national or social origin, property, birth or other status.

United Nations Universal Declaration of Human Rights
December 10, 1948

When I was about eleven years old, my mother, my pious Aunt Madeline, and I took a bus to a Catholic abbey somewhere in the New York Tri-State area. In one photo I took that day, my mom and aunt posed next to a life-sized statue of Francis of Assisi, the peacemaker and lover of all creation. In another shot, they sat in front of a statue of Anthony of Padua, an early Franciscan celebrated as the saint of lost things. In the image, Anthony stares adoringly into the eyes of the Christ Child. Over my mother's left shoulder is an outside staircase…

stairs I took that led to a shocking encounter I will never forget, one that further exposed me to the shameful reality of interracial life in America.

Decades later when I came across those pictures, I was absolutely astonished to see the staircase again, even though the memory of it was embedded in my gray matter. Gazing at the pictures, I was moved to wonder over the decision of a young boy to capture on film his family members with *these* saints from *that* vantage point.

———•———

At some point that day, I headed up the stairs tugging on the banister bordering the right side of the staircase. Eyes down, I focused on the stairs immediately ahead, always on the outlook for dropped treasures or coins. (Hey, as a city kid I knew folks dropped stuff all the time on the sidewalks and streets of our town.)

I peeked up once and realized a woman in a long, dark dress was coming down the stairs, directly in front of me. She apparently was also hugging the banister. Now, common courtesy and respect for my elders should have dictated I let go of the railing and swing left to let her pass.

But considering how much fun it was to tease adults— especially those I did not know—I decided to hang fast and see if she would go around me to my left. But that is not what happened. Eyes still down, about two steps prior to an inevitable collision, I watched her shoes stop and then shift to *her* left. She stepped *off* the concrete stairs and into the dirt on the side. I looked up in stunned disbelief then to discover this was *a* Black *woman!*

There I was, this dopey, white kid boppin' up the stairs with an attitude and not a care in the world. I was a child—a child who had just forced an adult African-American woman to step onto the ground off the side of the stairs. Who knew what prior humiliations this poor lady had experienced at the hands of white people? Unexpectedly, for both me and her, I had caused it to happen once again.

Memories flashed as I stared at the photos. Over the years, I've heard men sitting around bars sharing appalling stories about occasions where they insulted, humiliated, or terrorized African Americans by forcing them to step into the gutter or dirt as they passed by. (One boasted of ganging up with his friends on a black classmate and hanging him out a window by his legs.) The men at the bar laughed, they drank, they pounded their chests. For them, this was the way of the world. This was how you kept "them" in their place and in "their" own neighborhoods.

———•———

This harassed woman and I stood there looking at each other, she nervous and expectant; me in shock, grief, and embarrassment. I grilled myself with, "*Look what I did…look what I did… look what I just did!*" I wanted to say something like I did not mean for this to happen…that I'm not like that…that this was just a bad mistake. I muttered "I'm so sorry," pivoted to the left, and ran up those stairs into some foliage where I sat, caught my breath, and whimpered.

Most likely I told this tale to a priest in Confession, though I do not recall doing so; I do know I told no one else; not for years, probably not for decades. It was that moving and painful. Looking back, I ask myself why *this* incident took place *there* in the presence of Saint Francis and his followers. Perhaps it was a sign to me of how incomplete I was, how hard it would be to live my convictions, how difficult it would be to walk the talk.

Dare I also imagine that a bit of the sacred was trying to break through? The lesson was something like, *Look, kid, your heart is in the right place, but expect to screw up. This will not be the last time. But stay on the path; keep climbing those stairs; learn to back off; if you stumble, get back up and try to do better the next time.* Thinking about this now comforts me. But at that point I was too young and too inexperienced to think so deeply.

Fourth

—•—

Radical Priest

[We are] "Determined to promote and defend the Christian principles upon which our republic rests, principles of inalienable human rights, and equality before God."

The Constitution of the Sacred Heart Catholic Youth Organization, New Brunswick, New Jersey, circa 1963

"Late Louie Leyh," that's what folks called him, not because he was deceased; indeed, in the 1960s the Reverend Louis Anthony Leyh was very much alive and lively. He got the moniker because he was never on time for anything; not once, not ever.

In 1959, Father Louis Leyh became assistant pastor of Sacred Heart Church in New Brunswick. He was thirty-one years old and soon found himself serving as the Reverend Moderator for the parish's Catholic Youth Organization (CYO) and as chaplain for Catholics at nearby Douglas College, the women's campus of Rutgers University.

A graduate of St. Mary's Seminary, Emmitsburg, Maryland, this young, joyous priest was easy to be around. He was cheerful, a lover of theater, show tunes, classical music, and—much to our great joy—rock 'n roll. I'm serious about this last thing; under his watchful eye, our CYO accumulated an amazing collection of the most popular 45-RPM vinyl records. Of course, Fr. Leyh would not sign off on some of the more risqué titles, like the Coasters *Little Egypt,* about an exotic dancer. On the other hand, he did not blink an eye when we bought and played Brian Hyland's *Itsy Bitsy Teenie Weenie Yellow Polka-dot Bikini* (possibly because the protagonist was having conscience qualms over this particular fashion statement).

Fr. Leyh liked being around teenagers and young adults and showed great respect for us. You could talk and goof around with him about anything. To kids brought up in a rather stern, pre-Vatican II Catholic environment, he was a breath of fresh air; you had to love the guy, and we did.

The priest believed in expanding the horizons of young people and promoted participation in various social, cultural, athletic, and spiritual activities making up the sum and substance of our vibrant CYO. He encouraged kids to take leadership positions within the organization. Many answered the call, getting deeply involved in various projects. Some became officers in the local organization. Some of us organized fundraisers to buy records and audio equipment or to send busloads of kids to Broadway shows or other venues. Others planned, promoted, and ran our periodic Friday night dances. Sometimes, a hundred or more teenagers from the parish and the community attended those dances, which featured local or even more successful recording groups like the *Dovells* and the *Twilights*.

In CYO, we practiced what was called "lay leadership." We learned practical skills like doing mass mailings, marketing events, taking responsibility for projects and seeing them through, learning from our mistakes, and working to produce successful outcomes. This was practice and ownership you just did not get in high school. It was rich, rewarding, powerful training; and in my case, it prepared me for a lifetime of varied social justice struggles that lie ahead.

We elected officers annually and held monthly meetings, always using proper parliamentary procedures. The treasurer collected and deposited funds and disbursed payments after checks were signed by Father. Members voted on group activities as well as how funds would be spent or gifted. As I recall, except for rules regarding holding office, there were no upper class-lower class distinctions, no jocks or cool-kid elites as there were in high school. We were working-class and middle-class kids, the children of craftsmen, truck drivers, cops, office workers, and small businesspeople; teenagers who found a place that was of, by, and for us. Indeed, some of us decided to ignore what we saw as mundane, controlled after-school activities for the challenges, learning opportunities, and fun available to us through our CYO. We also learned, first-hand, about democracy and working as a team. For example, we wrote our group's constitution.

—•—

Some fifty years later, in total astonishment and with a smile of satisfaction, I can only ask, "Who were those kids…and who was that priest?"

To several of us, "Late Louie" was more than a spiritual

force; he was a teacher, a mentor, and a friend. Truth be told, annoying as it was to wait around for him, what he brought to the table was well worth waiting for.

Fr. Leyh had a mischievous, yet serious, political side. It might be an overstatement to call him "radical," but he certainly was progressive and spoke truth to power. For example, he often spoke of the civil rights struggles being waged by African Americans. This was nothing new to us; we saw it up close and personal in our neighborhoods and on television. Then, too, the Sisters in our schools constantly addressed discrimination and inequality in America, especially in the harsh "separate but equal" Jim Crow South.

What was so different in all this was Father Leyh's call to not only practice the Golden Rule in our interactions with minority groups but to learn as much as we could about the Civil Rights Movement and the struggles of the poor and marginalized.

In 1961, the Catholic author and journalist, John Howard Griffin, shocked white America with the publication of his best-selling book, *Black Like Me.* Griffin used investigative journalism and participant observation to send articles back to *Sepia Magazine* as he posed as a black man on a journey through the Deep South in 1959.

Masquerading as an African American proved to be no small feat. Griffin darkened his skin with the help of a dermatologist. He also exposed himself to ultraviolet rays using a sun lamp. Griffin then enhanced the pigmentation change with stain and shaved his head. Later, heeding the advice of a black confidant, he shaved his hands to complete the transformation.

One summer, Fr. Leyh arranged for us to attend a Tri-State CYO gathering in New York City. Incredibly, the agenda included a presentation by Griffin. Most of us had read *Black Like Me* in school, so there was a fair amount of excitement about going to hear this man talk about his adventures.

One evening we gathered in a conference room at the Sheraton Hotel. After a brief introduction and much to our surprise, a wheelchair-bound, partially paralyzed, and frail John Howard Griffin, rolled onto the stage. That stage usually hosted talks given by businesspeople and politicians. However, this night it was about to be transformed into something else: the stage as pulpit, as university, as a place of power and truth, of sadness and outrage, of struggle and hope.

The lights were dimmed; a single spotlight shone down on Mr. Griffin. He had no notes, books, or documents. He spoke only in monotone, in a deep yet powerful "radio" voice. The audience was locked in, attentive, silent. I remember being aware of this and was in awe of his command over us, because our group of generally antsy and raucous kids had a very short attention span.

Griffin spoke of the difficulties he had after his metamorphosis, how he had become unrecognizable even to himself when he looked in the mirror the first time following his treatments. The white John Howard Griffin had disappeared, he said, and for a time he struggled to understand who or what race he really was. He admitted to being scared, lonely, and full of doubts about his planned course of action. But he was determined to follow through with his research.

Griffin talked about the interactions he had with both black and white people on the streets of New Orleans and in Mississippi. He told of difficulties he had locating accommodations, where to eat, and safe places to rest or even use a restroom. He described incidents of harassment, insults, and silent stares; of encountering the language of disapproval, disrespectful treatment, and downright cruelty.

Then, too, he recalled courteous interactions he experienced from some white people. He even suggested that, on average, Southern whites were appalled by racist behaviors but often kept silent as they were afraid of retaliation by the KKK and other racists in their community.

Griffin spoke about the interactions he had after completing the project and returning home; how he and his family received death threats and how he was hung in effigy in his hometown of Mansfield, Texas.

I will never forget that event, Mr. John Howard Griffin's full name, what he did, his manner of speaking, and how moved I was by his brave witness. I was fascinated by his use of participant observation. Indeed, early in his book he wrote he considered this a research project, collecting and reporting data. This intrigued me and, in retrospect, had an impact on my later decision to study and work in the field of sociological research and evaluation.

I shook this man's hand before he took his leave. I was, at once, diminished and uplifted. Diminished, because who could possibly live up to a witness such as this? Uplifted because, in meeting this man, I had been exposed to true heroism. For me, here sat a man who embodied what it truly meant to be a patriot—defending Constitutional protections—and being a Catholic—applying your faith in the quest for social justice. It seemed, for the first time to me, that the saying "Saints do walk the Earth" was more than a cliché. Here was proof. For me, here was someone who modeled it.

Our good Father Leyh encouraged us to learn more about civil rights issues from the perspective of African Americans by engaging with local groups working to end discrimination and inequality. One of those groups was a local chapter of the Congress of Racial Equality (CORE), that had a storefront office across from the railroad station in downtown New Brunswick. CORE, we learned, was founded by James Farmer, a black man who promoted the techniques of Gandhian nonviolence. The group advocated civil disobedience using tactics such as sit-ins at lunch counters, picketing, and boycotting. The organization had offices in dozens of cities in the North and South.

I suspect Father Leyh was interested in this group because it advocated nonviolence, which grew out of Farmer's earlier work with the Fellowship of Reconciliation, a confederation of religious based peace groups, including the Catholic Peace Fellowship.

One time, I decided to head downtown to attend a CORE meeting. I cannot remember if I went with anyone or much about the actual meeting. I do know I was welcomed warmly and handed a black button that simply read 'CORE' with a white equal sign under the lettering. Buttons with political statements were becoming more popular at the time, though few people, other than the young, wore them. I remember wearing this one in solidarity from time to time.

I was sixteen years old and still under a curfew. It got dark. I checked my watch and, although the meeting was still going on, headed home. The next morning, I walked by the CORE office to find the huge storefront window was cracked top to bottom.

Overnight, someone had broken the glass. This disgraceful act, this violent reaction to folks exercising their rights of peaceful assembly, affected me more than anything that had been said at the meeting.

I saw firsthand something of the degree of anger and resentment that could be directed toward the black community. Here. In New Jersey. Of course, I was well aware of the verbal insults, the stories of harassment, the indignities suffered by African Americans in our community, but this incident was different, because the night before I had been part of that meeting—me, a visitor, a seeker, a white boy.

I remember standing there looking at the glass, a cracked reflection staring back at shattered hopes of a naïve young boy who was taking initial steps toward social action. This teenager, who stood up for his black buddies and challenged the prejudices of adults and was embarrassed when he unintentionally compelled a black woman to move off the steps onto the dirt to let her pass, had never truly understood the degree of hatred and fear behind the insults and discrimination until the Griffin talk and the CORE meeting. I remember feeling disillusioned, disappointed, and somewhat sad. Naively I thought, *Who does this? What would they do next?*

It was then I realized violence directed toward one portion of the community is actually violence directed toward all of us. This powerful, terrifying, shocking epiphany, once stillborn, became flesh … and gradually quickened within me.

———•———

These were the years when John F. Kennedy assumed the presidency, when Dorothy Day was standing up against the proliferation of nuclear weapons, when the civil rights movement was in full bloom, when the U.S. intervention in Vietnam was still a dirty little secret.

Father Leyh, like all of us, was overjoyed with the election of Kennedy, the Catholic. As proud Catholic-Americans we believed in this modern-day Lancelot who would bring Camelot to America. We all trusted what were dubbed "the Best and the Brightest" in the Kennedy administration, who promoted detente with the Russians and in common-sense programs like the Peace Corps, led by another Catholic in-law of the Kennedys, Sargent Schriver.

At the time, I knew virtually nothing about Thomas Merton, the Secular-Franciscan then Trappist monk who was writing brilliant missives against war and nuclear weapons from his cell in the Abbey of Our Lady of Gethsemani. I did know a little about Dorothy Day because she labored in one of her Catholic-Worker houses of hospitality a mere forty miles away in Manhattan.

Revealing a little of his radical side, Father Leyh told us about the Catholic Worker Movement, its history, mission, and newspaper, *The Catholic Worker*. He noted the paper was still a penny a copy some thirty years after it launched. (The price is still the same in 2022, more than eighty years since its first issue!)

As kids, we were forced to participate in what were called "duck and cover" civil-defense drills at school. Here we were trained to move away from windows, duck under desks, and cover our heads, told this would help protect us in the unlikely event of a nuclear bomb. Since these periodic exercises in the absurd occupied a good chuck of class time, we kids were happy to go through the motions. I was a lot less excited about the periodic, compulsory, after school air-raid drills that required folks to get off the streets and seek shelter. My feeling was, *"Hey, this is America. The government does not get to tell us to get off the streets. I have newspapers to deliver!"*

Soon we were very excited to learn from Father Leyh that Dorothy Day and her companions were refusing to get off the streets during the fifteen-minute, legally enforced air-raid drills. I thought, *Hey, she's willing to go to jail to get her newspapers out.* Joking aside, we understood her witness was really about banning the bomb and working for a nuclear free world. A gutsy position, that. And it worked. Between 1955 and 1961, civil disobedience to air raid drills increased and the drills eventually ended.

———•———

With enthusiasm and great expectations, our Reverend Moderator Leyh once placed copies of *The Catholic Worker* on the literature rack in the narthex of Sacred Heart Church. This turned out to be the first and only time our parishioners got to see that particular publication on that particular rack. Somebody complained and our pastor made Fr. Leyh take them out. Apparently, the pastor was under pressure from folks who thought the Catholic Worker Movement was somehow less-than-Catholic, socialist, and downright anti-American.

This incident got our young brains attention. How could a decidedly Catholic organization, clearly involved in peacemaking and works of mercy, scare adults and clerics to a point where they just wanted *The Catholic Worker* newspaper—if not the organization—to disappear?

I have to admit raging hormones, our quest for fun (broadly defined), and the pressures of high school conspired against most of us when it came to thinking deeply about this and other problems of the world. However, many of my generation had a deep and developing social consciousness, so the attack on something that meant so much to Fr. Leyh was disturbing. Even here, with only a moral victory to hang his hat on, he taught us something. You are not always going to win; winning is not what it is all about (despite Vince Lombardi's famous quote of the time). It's about witness, doing the next right thing, taking one step forward even if you are beaten two steps back. It's about speaking truth to power, even when you must step away from confrontation and surrender to win another day in as dignified and gentle a way as you can.

Given our age and immediate concerns, perhaps the best we could do was to file this frustrating experience away in the vast amphitheater of our developing brains. I certainly did, not knowing frustration and failure would rise again with a vengeance in a time soon to come. A time when adolescence would abruptly be stolen from our generation as we, like our parents and grandparents before us, were forced into adulthood at the mercy of a war. This time, ten million of us mostly Christian soldiers were locked and loaded, armed to the teeth, and told to be ready to "kill a Commie for Christ."

Fifth

———•———

The Year of the Monkey

Coming to terms with things our conscience cannot
approve means that we must share the responsibility
for them because they have our assent.

Rev. Alfred Delp, S.J.

By 1968, over 19,560 United States soldiers had been killed
in Vietnam. Another 16,592 would die in Southeast Asia
in 1968, and another 11,616 in 1969—the two highest annual
totals during the war. As the war raged on, racial and other tensions turned violent in cities and on campuses throughout the
country; antiwar protesters burned their draft card; and students and faculty organized opposition to the war on college
campuses nationwide.

Meanwhile, draft-aged men throughout the country sought
ways to confront or avoid the draft. Some successfully enlisted in
the National Guard, thereby avoiding being sent overseas. Many
tried to delay their conscription by applying for deferments

or by seeking medical, hardship, education, divinity, or other exemptions from military service. Estimates varied wildly, but upwards of 30,000 young men, some with families, chose to leave the country and reside in Canada. For patriotic or altruistic reasons, or to avoid being drafted, others decided to enlist in one branch of the military or another. Doing so lengthened their service time, but it also offered a chance to choose what was called a "Military Occupational Specialty" more to their liking.

———•———

Throughout 1968, President Lyndon Johnson, Secretary of Defense Robert McNamara, General William Westmoreland, and others in the federal government were having a very tough time convincing the public the war was going well and victory was in sight. The unexpected Tet Offensive of January-February of that year saw the Viet Cong (VC) and the North Vietnamese Army (NVA) unleash a massive offensive against South Vietnam, including an attack on the U.S. Embassy in Saigon. The fighting was fierce, exploding the myth the Communist forces were on the run and unable to conduct large-scale military operations. Ultimately the VC and NVA were beaten back at the time, but the U.S. government and military leaders were shocked by the power and extent of the assault. There was also a noticeable shift in the already cautious support for the war as a stunned U.S. public saw what was really happening and largely turned against the war. According to polls, approximately half the country now thought going into Vietnam had been a mistake.

Anti-draft sit-ins and demonstrations increased on college campuses, with students sometimes closing down classes or taking over buildings. They demanded an immediate end to the war and the presence of ROTC (Reserve Officers Training Corps) on campus. President Johnson, who was confronting antiwar primary challenges by Eugene McCarthy and Robert Kennedy, decided not to run for re-election by the end of March.

Over and above this anger and disillusionment with the war, the nation wept in response to the April 1968 assassination of Reverend Martin Luther King, Jr., in Memphis. In addition to his struggle for racial equality and civil liberties, King had started to speak out against the war. His death further fueled racial tensions and African-American opposition to the war in Vietnam. Widespread rioting occurred in American cities including Newark, New Jersey, near my hometown of New Brunswick.

In May that year, Jesuit priests Daniel and his brother Phillip Berrigan, along with seven other Catholic and Christian antiwar activists, raided the Selective Service Office in Catonsville, Maryland. They grabbed over 300 draft records and burned them in the parking lot. A few weeks later, presidential candidate Robert F. Kennedy, brother of the assassinated President John F. Kennedy, was assassinated in Los Angeles, California, after winning the California presidential primary.

People in my age group (18-30) had never-ending conversations about ways to resist the draft and organize opposition to the war. Culturally, this was reinforced by the vibrant antiwar folk music of Woody Guthrie and his son Arlo, Pete Seeger, Joan Baez, Peter, Paul, and Mary, and others. In addition, music of the post-World War II baby boom generation quickly and radically changed as Rock-n-Roll, Gospel, and the Blues produced the likes of Bob Dylan, Stevie Wonder, Janice Joplin, Jimmie Hendrix, and numerous "super-groups" who sang songs of love, resistance, and societal change. It was our time, our music, our culture, and—shockingly—our war.

———•———

Many people used all the familiar patriotic and nonviolent civil rights methods available to bring our grievances to the government and to educate the public. We wrote letters to the editor, to the President, and to our Congresspeople, sometimes visiting the latter in small groups. Folks put out "alternative" newspapers and fliers, held local rallies and vigils, and sometimes attended regional or national marches for peace. Around the country, many students joined various campus antiwar groups, usually to gather peacefully seeking an end to the war, but occasionally taking over campus buildings or being arrested for acts of civil disobedience in towns and cities. Doctors, teachers, clergy, and other professionals increasingly spoke out against the war. Groups like the Women's Strike for Peace and Mothers for Peace appeared on the national scene. The Southern Christian Leadership Conference (SCLC) and the Student Nonviolent Coordinating Committee (SNCC), so active in civil rights issues, now openly proclaimed their opposition to the war. The Students for a Democratic Society (SDS) and the Black Panthers staked out positions on the radical left. By the late 1960s, these civilian groups were also joined by Vietnam Era veterans, especially members of the Vietnam Veterans Against the War (VVAW). For the most part, young people like me viewed all this as a celebration of what grass-roots democracy looked like and what so many of us believed in and lived.

Most of us were uninformed when it came to the draft, however. Violating the Selective Service Act could lead to up to five years in prison and a fine of up to $10,000. We knew that at age eighteen all males were required to register for the draft. Except for those who publicly resisted registration, went underground or left the country, this was what all men did. (Registration for the draft is still required today, still only for men.)

Following registration, everyone had an opportunity to file for deferments or exemptions through their local Selective Service office. Registrants had to be deemed physically and mentally fit per standards established by the Defense Department before they could be inducted into military service.

There were numerous deferments and exemptions: some public officials, members in the National Guard and the Military Reserve, full-time students attending high school or college, ministers and divinity students, those working in various occupations like agriculture or in certain industries, and those in certain marital or familial situations. Deferments and exemptions were also available for many medical and psychological conditions.

Briefly, the process of getting inducted involved completion of what was called an initial "Classification Questionnaire," the provision of medical or other documentation, an initial physical examination, and, if no deferment or exemptions were granted, a final physical at the time of possible induction into the military.

There was also a very controversial exemption for Conscientious Objection (C.O.) status, sometimes but not always granted to members of sects known as "peace churches"—especially the Mennonites, the Religious Society of Friends (Quakers), and the Church of the Brethren. Registrants belonging to the more mainstream Christian traditions, including Catholicism, found it very difficult to obtain conscientious objector status. By the late 1960s, C.O. status was being granted to those whose "religious training and belief" led them to be opposed to all war. However, registrants who held beliefs that were political, academic, or based on a selective opposition to a particular war were still not eligible.

There were two categories of conscientious objection considered by the Selective Service System. A registrant could request "I-O" draft status. If approved by the draft board, that person served for two years in a nonprofit facility, like a hospital. During the 1960s and depending on the draft board, I-O status was almost impossible to get.

Potential draftees could also apply for the second option, classification "I-A-O." In this case, a person was drafted into the military but served with noncombatant status. These draftees would not be subjected to the handling or use of weapons. However, they would attend Basic Training to learn everything else: marching, decorum, organization, etc. After basic training, these men would generally head over to medical school at Fort Sam Houston to become medics. In the 1960s, orders to go to Vietnam soon followed.

Draft boards, if they were enlightened enough to even consider a claim for conscientious objection, were more likely to grant I-A-O noncombatant status because the man *was* drafted and counted toward fulfilling the system's draft quota for a particular month. I-O conscientious objectors did not.

At eighteen years old, I pondered long and hard over applying for either conscientious objector status, especially for "I-O." I even had the application form sent to me. It is true the non-combatant service option was an appealing compromise; that is, I could follow my conscience, state my opposition to the war, but still enter the military. However, like many others I came to believe a conscripted non-combatant would still be helping to prosecute the war. At that point, I no longer saw non-combatant conscientious objection as an honorable way for me to proceed. Moreover, I concluded that in good conscience I could not truthfully answer some of the questions being asked in the questionnaire. For example, I struggled with the requirement an applicant be opposed to "war in *every* form." The fact was I just did not know enough to say yes to that. I didn't know anyone who was a C.O. or even anyone trained to help me think these questions through. Ultimately, I decided neither classification was right for me and came to believe the questions and the process were really a set-up stacked in favor of the system, aimed at getting people to do exactly what I did … not apply for conscientious-objector status of any kind.

I did return all the other forms and documentation requested, along with a statement declaring I was opposed to the Vietnam War. I also discussed my position with the doctors at the preliminary physical, who of course medically passed me with flying colors. One, as I recall, offered some backhanded support for my opposition to the war writing a paraphrase something like, "You probably don't want this guy in situations with other soldiers who want to be there."

For a year or so, I had a student deferment while attending a junior college near my home. After two years, though, I got bored with it as it replicated much of the ground we covered in Catholic high school. The ambitious older teenager I was then also simply wanted to get on with life, and I naïvely believed I could take on the Selective Service System and be exempted from the military based on my specific opposition to the Vietnam War.

I dropped out of college and got married in February 1968, four months after turning twenty. I knew others who were doing the same thing I was—making an adolescent decision to live some type of a regular life while living under the cloud of being called up to serve in the war. Some couples planned to have a child immediately, while the exemption for married parents still existed, but many of us could not go down this route. It just did not seem to be either an appropriate way to start a family or a fitting way to stand up to the draft.

So, it was "game on" for me with the Selective Service System. Of course, the system won. At least initially.

Sixth

—•—

Induction Station

"I, _____, do solemnly swear (or affirm) that I will support and defend the Constitution of the United States against all enemies, foreign and domestic; that I will bear true faith and allegiance to the same; and that I will obey the orders of the President of the United States and the orders of the officers appointed over me, according to regulations and the Uniform Code of Military Justice. So help me God."

Oath of Enlistment Title 10, US Code; effective 5 October 1962

On July 3, 1968, I arrived at the Armed Forces Examining and Entrance Station in Newark, New Jersey. I had spent the preceding days writing an essay detailing my reasons for opposing the war in Vietnam and why I felt I should not participate. All of twenty years old, I naïvely believed this document would, once and for all, convince those in charge that my opposition to the war was real; they would find me administratively unacceptable; and they would send me home.

I'll tell you what; it certainly got their attention. After handing it in, I was told to go through a final physical examination with the others and wait for further instructions. So there we were, all these naked guys spreading their buttocks and being asked to cough while medical professionals held their balls and checked for hernias, diseases, and abnormalities: an assembly line of naked boys, all in the early stages of being disassembled and reconstructed. Nobody looked anybody else in the eye. Discussing it later, I found many felt embarrassed and dehumanized, like cattle being herded to the slaughter. It seemed to me that everyone who had thus far navigated the Selective Service System without getting deferred or exempted passed the physical with flying colors.

I was singled out and told to report to an office across the hall. Here I met the officer in charge (O.C.), who made it very clear he was not too happy having someone upset his otherwise well-oiled machine. He said something like, "I read your document; you need to go see our shrink and come back to see me." Standard practice I later learned, but can you imagine? It was as if anyone who challenged the war had to be out of their minds.

The shrink and I had a pleasant conversation as he evaluated my status to determine if I suffered from any mental diseases that would disqualify me from military service. I was found to be coherent and able to distinguish the difference between right and wrong … and therefore qualified for induction into the Army.

He asked why I had not filed for conscientious objector status with my draft board. I told him I got the paperwork, but I did not complete it or send it in because I had trouble signing off on one of the statements asking me to agree I was "opposed to war in any form." (World War II, for example, was often cited as a just war and I was well aware of the horrors, death, and destruction fascism brought to the world and why peoples and nations rose up to stop it.)

I was also aware of the Catholic Church's teaching called the "Just War" theory. This teaching does not completely repudiate warfare; however, believers were taught they could use this set of standards to decide if participation in a particular war was justified. But the secular authorities did not subscribe to the notion of selective objection to a particular war. To be classified as a conscientious objector, you had to be opposed to war in any form. Again, I struggled mightily with that teaching as a potential draftee, but decided I could not meet that standard, and I was not going to lie.

Finally, the shrink scribbled a diagnosis that qualified me for induction; under it he wrote a warning: "The man will follow this through."

———•———

So, there I was, healthy and apparently not crazy, back in the office with the O.C. He was very upset as he asked, "I need to know if you are going to refuse to be inducted. Remember, if you do you will be arrested and tried for refusing induction, a violation of the Universal Training and Service Act." He continued, "If you are going to refuse, I want you to do it here, not out there in front of the rest of the guys."

I was not there to make a scene, although some other inductees periodically showed up for induction and did just that. I certainly was not astute or radical enough to realize the impact such a public demonstration of resistance might have on the other inductees in the room; but apparently the O.C. was. He sure did not want it to happen that day on his watch. One thing I learned from the Civil Rights Movement was presenting a vision of society that ran contrary to accepted norms makes those in power very uncomfortable, perhaps even fearful. I saw a powerful example of this here.

At this point the O.C. became a bit more "fatherly," suggesting a number of guys came through having problems with the war, saying that was not so unusual. He knew others had difficulty taking the Oath of Enlistment or any oath; that is, swearing in front of God. He said all one needed to do was say, "I affirm" rather than "I swear" and simply take a step forward when told to do so.

He said, "Look, you are obviously an intelligent and thoughtful guy; you've got two years of college under your belt; that means something. Once you get to Fort Dix, they'll give you all these aptitude tests to see how best to use you." He continued, "The military is not just killing, blood and guts, you know. It takes a lot of support staff to run an efficient army. They can use a guy like you in any number of jobs."

I remember sitting there with my head down, tired of all the dealings with Selective Service, tired of presenting a case nobody in power wished to recognize, tired with what felt like an endless battle to get more people to look at the Vietnam War—to really look at the *Vietnam* War—and to take action to do something about it.

And then, the coup de grace. "And there's another thing young man. I see you are recently married. Even if the marriage survives, how the hell are you going to provide for your family after a felony conviction and a possible $10,000 fine after serving a three-to-five-year sentence? Who the hell is going to take a chance on you, a draft-dodger, an ex-con? So, c'mon, let's get this over with."

So now it was crunch time. I tallied up the ledger. I had not dodged the draft by doing anything illegal, though I understood the motives of those who did. I refused to pack up and leave the country, stubbornly insisting the fight to end the war was here (though I admired the courage and commitment it took for others to move permanently to Canada or elsewhere). I did not decide to join the National Guard or Reserves as a way to avoid being drafted (though I knew many who did and truly respected their decision). Finally, I had great respect for those who entered the service firmly believing the war was necessary, legal, and just.

There were only two options open: refuse induction and go to prison, or agree to be inducted. I had immense respect for those who refused to compromise their beliefs and went to jail for refusing to be inducted. In that minute, however, I did not think I could be one of them. I have to admit I was afraid to go to prison. It rubbed against everything I had been taught and internalized—"keep your nose clean," "play by the rules," "stay out of trouble," and so on. In truth, I was also angry that otherwise law-abiding men who opposed what many considered an illegal and immoral war had to be imprisoned for their beliefs.

I once had a student deferment and I *chose* to drop out of college and take my chances with the draft; nobody forced me. I got the conscientious objector paperwork from Selective Service. However, without the support needed to work through the notion of being opposed to war in any form I took what I thought was the high road and did not send it in.

It seemed as if I'd been walking down the same street and constantly running into the same dead end. Perhaps I was wrong, but I knew I needed to go down another path. Feeling distraught, dropping the ball, and in Christian terms failing to pick up my cross, I finally muttered to the O.C., "Okay...okay. I'll affirm."

I was aching inside; confused and defeated, I joined the rest of the group on the thick, plush, burgundy carpet covering the induction-room floor. The O. C. read the Oath of Enlistment out loud. When he came to, "I will support and defend the **Constitution of the United States** against all enemies, foreign **and domestic,**" my head jerked to attention and I began to get off my pity-pot. It was a click moment, one when, like flipping a switch, the darkness suddenly surrenders to the light.

Many of us knew the Vietnamese people posed no threat to our country—we were not defending our country from attack. The conflict did not appear to be constitutional, since Congress had abdicated its responsibility by not formally declaring war— they surely were not upholding or defending the Constitution of the United States. So, I rationalized if the enemies were not foreign, then they just might be domestic folks who had promoted this war by choice and gotten us into this mess. Perhaps, just perhaps, I could do something to end the war within the system, within the military service. Probably not the best plan, but in that moment, it lifted my spirits and gave me hope.

———•———

As we walked out the door to the bus to take us to the Reception Center at Fort Dix, New Jersey, we encountered a tall, serious-looking young man handing out New Testaments. He did not say anything like "Good luck" or "God bless." This was no Bible-thumping evangelist on a soapbox; no self-serving Elmer

Gantry preying on people. He just stood there, dour and silent, handing out books as one might deal cards during a tense and critical hand of poker. He did not say, "Repent!" or, on the other hand, "Turn back, don't get on that bus!" He just handed out books. I expected to hear the unspoken refrain, "onward Christian soldier!" escape from his lips. At least that is how I took it; I was mad and feeling spiritually abandoned. I stopped, looked him dead in the eye, and said, "How dare you? How could you?" As he reached out once again to hand me the Good Book, I threw up my hand in disgust, took the final few steps, and got on the bus...I was in the army now.

Seventh

—●—

The Wheels on the Bus

A regular guy can handle anything.

Rev. Alfred Delp, S.J.

There was absolute silence on the bus, except for the occasional melancholy sigh or muffled sob; a mausoleum on wheels, a charter bus to the unfathomable. I took a seat roughly midway down the aisle that gave me a good view of the rest of the bus. As others entered, I saw most of the men were my age or younger, kids eighteen to twenty years old, with a sprinkling of guys somewhat older; but none were older than twenty-six, the cutoff for induction into the Army.

For the most part, eyes were lowered, brows tense, lips taut, arms often crossed over rib cages, holding in the pain, trying to ignore the fear, fighting back the tears lest someone notice. Once seated, some seemed numb, confronting what seemed to be a thoroughly irrational situation. Few expressed anything resembling pride in their situation. After all, they had been drafted and had not enlisted; if anything, they seemed to be simply resigned to their fate. Nobody seemed "at ease," a phrase we would come to know all too well in the next few days.

I could not help but wonder: *Who were these guys? Where were they from? What were they like? How did they perceive the war, the draft, and being drafted? Did any consider they had a choice other than to enlist or be drafted? How many considered military service as some sort of essential public duty? Was it considered a masculine rite of passage? Did they suspect their years in the army would predominantly feature "Fun, Travel, and Adventure" as the recruiters might promise?*

Was it possible some equated conscription with some modern version of "Indentured Servitude"—that is, surrendering both their freedom and earning power in return for public admiration, status, and perhaps good jobs in the future? Or had they seen conscription as something to be avoided at all costs, but ultimately accepted if that fateful "Greetings from the Selective Service" letter arrived? How many had applied for exemptions or deferments prior to being called to military service? How many were either denied legitimate claims for exemption or did not know they might have qualified for one?

Were any of them questioning the morality or politics of the war in Vietnam? How many were truly opposed to this war? Who among them had serious doubts about the war, their willingness to fight it, or believed their country was truly threatened by the Vietnamese? Who amongst us would stand up against the war—and how could this be done?

Perhaps seeking soulmates, I pondered these questions as they continued to spin around in my head and soul. Willingly or unwillingly, we had all just left home, loved ones, perhaps parents, siblings, spouses, girlfriends. Some left jobs. Some left school. Like it or not, we were all now members of the U.S.

military, most of us in one form or another to become veterans of that era. Veterans of the war itself and/or veterans of the war-against-the-war.

Whatever our thoughts, experiences, or perspectives, I came to understand this: All of us were leaving behind the past; that was then, and this was now. The future was uncertain. In reality, for some, the future would not last much longer. Still, nobody wanted to believe he would die.

As we left the city and cruised the New Jersey Turnpike, some guys, myself included, stared blankly out the windows; our first experience of what combat veterans call "the thousand-yard stare." Some guys slept as the scenery changed from urban to suburban into what was left of rural southern New Jersey, past the green and open space of the Pine Barrens to Fort Dix. I took to watching the cars go by and gazing into the windows at the people going about their daily routines. The words to the popular Simon and Garfunkel song *America* came to mind, "They've all come to look for America." Indeed, so were we; and many of us on the bus were "empty and aching," knowing perfectly well just why.

If other drivers noticed us at all, chances are they thought we were a bunch of young guys on an excursion to some entertainment or sports venue. Nobody who saw us really cared; indeed, the only people on the entire length of the Turnpike who gave a damn about that behemoth barreling along at 60+ MPH were those of us who were on it. Why should it be otherwise? Yet, in that minute it just seemed to me that it should.

Now and again a car would go by and I would be blessed with snapshots of girls in mini-skirts or shorts speeding to points unknown; bare legs transporting me back to some of what was grand and glorious in the world. "The manifest miracle of women," Jeff Porteous, a prisoner of conscience whom I would come to know, once said.

After a while, I noticed some of the guys had loosened up a bit. I could hear snippets of hushed conversation rising above the din of tires reverberating over sun-soaked asphalt. I heard no laughing, but the sighs and sobs had stopped as men settled in. Guys behind me were spreading a rumor that ten percent of us were going to be separated out and sent to Parris Island to train as Marines. A couple guys reacted to this with something like, "Bullshit. If they choose me, I'm walking away. It ain't gonna happen." I found this remarkable, if not encouraging. I thought, wouldn't it be something if many of us just said "No" to the Marines? Indeed, "No" to the whole idea of conscription? Clearly, I was not alone in having doubts about the war and what we were being forced to do.

The small talk continued: "Where are you from? How old are you? Are you married? Do you have a girlfriend?" So much of it was the stuff of everyday life; guys taking the chance to get out of themselves. Still, the wheels on the bus rolled on... and on.

PART II

━━■●■━━

Maggot Days—Basic

How many of the guys on the bus, or the millions of others who entered the military during those years *really* knew what to expect? Nobody told us. Not family members who had served. Not the teachers in the class-room. Not the preachers in the pulpit—too many of whom sometimes endorsed and blessed killing "Godless Commies for Christ." Not the veterans from the World Wars or Korea who were notoriously closed-lipped about it. Not my brother who volunteered and did Marine Basic Training at Parris Island in the 1950s. Decades later, during the final, hazy days before his death he recalled his military experience and said to me, "Tell your family not to do it; they treat you like an animal."

In my experience, when kids or adults ask veterans about military events, the vets find ways to disengage or dismiss their involvement as something not worth discussing—something dark and taboo, something they had put behind them. If they discuss it at all the emphasis rarely seems to be about the train-ing. All things considered; perhaps basic training was a military experience all too many veterans viewed as small potatoes.

Eighth

──•◄──

Reception Center

I sighed and you heard me,
I wavered, and you steadied me.
I travelled along the broad way of the world,
but you did not desert me.

Augustine of Hippo

Later that Wednesday afternoon, we arrived at the Reception
Center at Fort Dix, New Jersey. As we drove in, the base
seemed abandoned; unknown to us at first, most officers, Cadre,
and non-trainees had left for a four-day Fourth of July holiday.
The base was being run with a skeleton crew of guys who really
did not want to be there; generally, screw-ups who had been
denied leave and those with essential jobs who were ordered to
stay.

Much later, we learned many of the guys assigned to basic
training units were veterans back from Vietnam; "short-timers,"
with a few months left on their enlistment or induction. They

were counting the days until discharge. When their time in service got down to days, guys were said to be "so short they could parachute off a dime." Many of these men were clearly fed up with the military. They were angry and bitter about having to wait to be discharged after what they had already seen, done, and survived while deployed in Southeast Asia. Many seemed heartsick and bone tired. Not only were they sick and tired, they were bored and uninspired. Here, in this place, the last thing they wanted to do was to continue to take orders and work with raw recruits. But, on day one, we conscripts did not know this.

Suddenly, the bus door opened, and all hell broke loose. Most of us did not know the meaning of the insignia on their sleeves, but it was worn by a couple of ragged looking Spec. 4s[1] who were screaming for us to get off the bus: cursing, shoving, and belittling guys as they stumbled out. "I want you 'maggots' off the bus, NOW!"

My mind wondered as we stumbled off the bus…*Maggots? Come again? What is that? You guys equate us with smarmy, flesh-eating, wormlike creatures?*

I raced through a list of invectives, expletives, and insults most of us in some form or another suffered while growing up. But this one was new; in my mind, "maggot" was something different, something dark, something sinister, something reeking and corrupted. I thought, *Beyond the insult and the degradation, what was this about? Was it a sticks-and-stones thing or some kind of mind game? A demeaning slur used to reinforce the idea that they were kings of the anthill and at any time we deserved to be crushed under their feet? I did not know. What I did know was the more people are put down, called stupid or worthless, the more likely they are*

---

[1] Specialist 4th Class, equivalent to a Corporal.

to live up to those epithets. I also knew that with self-doubt and low self-esteem, we often begin to accept the judgments of others, to begin to think that way, then to act that way. "Maggots?" Flesh destroying creatures… is this how they really saw us?

———•———

"Hurry up! Shut up! Line-up!" Each barked command was accompanied by an astounding array of profanity, F-words predominantly, along with attacks on our masculinity that equated us with female genitalia and/or oral sexual acts—homophobic or otherwise.

All the guys on the bus were exhausted, most apprehensive, many disillusioned, some docile and compliant. A few were clearly terrified, looking much like petrified fawns panicked and powerless in oncoming traffic. Some seemed angry… as angry as those who were bullying us. The still popular World War I song came to mind: "You're in the army now, you're not behind the plow. You'll never get rich, you sonofabitch, you're in the army now."

I mused, *well, what did "maggots" like us expect, a bloody Welcome Wagon?* Then, a different, fanciful scenario came to mind. *What if a couple of sharply dressed officers in Dress Greens had reached out to shake each guy's hand as they got off the bus?*

My thoughts morphed into a pipe dream. Perhaps those fantasy officers might say something like, *Happy to see you guys. We need you. For the next eight weeks our Drill Instructors will teach you the skills you will need to be the best you can be in this army. Every inductee is trained in weaponry, tactics, and the law of land warfare; although not all of you will be assigned to infantry or artillery Military Occupational Specialties. Basic military training is*

what we do here, and everybody goes through it. Expect Basic to be
tough and challenging, but by the time you get out of here you will
be in great shape, highly skilled in drill, and familiar with weaponry
and military procedures. We know it has been a tough day so line up
over there and we'll get you checked in, fed, and settled.

———•———

Excellent personnel management skills, don't you think? Trust
me, I understand the incongruity of this fantasy; but remember,
this was *minute one* of my military life! Much earlier, I had taken
a series of psychology and management courses in college.
Then, working in restaurant management, I knew screaming,
insulting, or blaming did not work and was counterproductive.
From my perspective, during my short career I learned to mold a
collection of teens, moonlighting adults, and retirees into a successful, well-oiled machine. So even at my young age, I understood things about motivation, teamwork, unit cohesion, and
playing to peoples' strengths while challenging them to learn
and acquire new skills. Basic training, I could see, was to be the
opposite.

The popular perspective might insist, "Yeah, right. That stuff
might play well in the civilian sector, but it is exactly this way of
thinking and behaving that has to be undone. Think about it. The
army gets all kinds of kids: good kids, smart kids, rogues, rascals,
slow kids, street punks, and down-home country boys. The military must break them all down, rewrite the rules of behavior,
instill unquestioned discipline, and rebuild them all into soldiers.
So, listen kid, Basic is not like going to football camp."

Some guys actually believed that. Guys would say things
like, "Hey, it can't be worse than what I went through with

Coach So-And-So." Others said, "It's just going to be a bunch of exercise, physical training, marching, and drill, what's so tough about that?" Or simply, "How bad can it be?"

Who knew? Bottom line, nobody knew. For now, let me admit to being shocked, indeed appalled, at this initial introduction to things military. Yup, I was very naïve. Simply put, except for what we learned from the movies, most of us were.

After lining up we were herded into an immense room bordered by tables overflowing with olive-drab fatigue uniforms, caps, socks, underwear, and boots. The screams and insults continued as we were ordered to sit on the floor in a wide circle while clothes were distributed. A small team of bored and extremely annoyed troops were assigned to handle distribution. If you knew your sizes, they told you where to pick up your new wardrobe; if you did not know your sizes, you were told to guess. In all cases we were commanded to "hurry the (bleep) up, shut the (bleep) up, and sit the (bleep) back down on the floor."

While this was happening, I was able to get a good look at my fellow inductees anchored to the floor, compliant in this circle of surrender. Most were white; probably working-class kids from the cities and suburbs of Northern and Central New Jersey, like me. These seemed to be the sons of craftsmen and factory workers, the "salt of the earth," as my dad would have described them. I guessed some of the older white guys were college educated and had received draft deferments during their college and graduate school years. Like legions of others, they may have been avoiding the draft in the hope the war would end before they graduated or they turned twenty-six.

A fair number of guys were African American, and a few were Hispanics. Most, I surmised, were plucked out of urban enclaves along with others from smaller cities. These cities and towns seemed to be undergoing a change in demographics brought on, in part, by urban riots and so-called "white flight" from the cities to the suburbs. Jobs, too, were disappearing as factories and businesses were moving away from urban centers. Were these guys poor? Possibly. Working-class? Mostly. Powerless? Absolutely.

Some of the guys were clearly out of shape; others just lanky and awkward. Some had a look of defiance. You saw it in the strut, the body language, the smirks and demeanor. These were street-smart kids, the bad boys…all present and accounted for. This was us; all of us, sitting in silence, mostly doe-eyed and edgy.

I wondered who among this group wanted to be there. How many believed the war to be right and just. How many for personal or patriotic reasons were willing, if not anxious, to serve. It was not yet apparent. There certainly were many. On the other hand, I would soon discover a significant number of guys who did not truly believe in the war.

At one point, postcards and pens were distributed during an expletive laden lecture that went something like:

- "You will address the front of the postcard to your parents or family member…you will do it now!
- "You will turn the card over and tell your people you have arrived safely and how happy you are to be here… you will not whine or complain like the group of pathetic little girls you are!"
- "You collection of miserable momma's boys will be in a world of pain if my Company Commander gets a call from her saying she hasn't heard from you!"

- "You will hand back my pens, all of my pens…you will not steal pens from my army. If one is missing none of you maggots will enter my mess hall for chow!"

I cannot remember what I wrote, but I'm sure my rushed, crisp note was reassuring. Soon, postcards and pens were returned; we were ordered to hurry-up and change into fatigues, gather up our stuff and run—not walk—to the mess hall. Oh yeah, this man's army paid the postage for the postcards.

Ninth

———•———

Hurry Up and Wait

So I boiled with anger, sighed, wept, and was at my wits' end.
I found no calmness, no capacity for deliberation.

Augustine of Hippo

The first night, we were left alone for much of the evening, told to expect a morning formation and the assignment of some cleanup tasks. Each barracks building seemed to have an unhappy and perpetually angry Spec 4 in a room at the far end of the barracks. We chose places among the bunk beds and tossed our personal belongings on the sides of the beds or into footlockers located at the foot of each bunk. Exhausted by the events of the day, most of us fell asleep rather quickly, the occasional muffled sob or sigh a melancholy lullaby periodically ushering the rest of us to sleep.

In the morning, the disagreeable rogue who was our barracks monitor woke us up to screams, curses, and insults as the shocked and often frightened troops piled off our beds. The Spec

4 advised us our mothers were not here, so we were to make our beds quicker than ASAP. Most of the guys had absolutely no idea how to do this. Actually, the entire exercise was really about doing things quickly and to point out just how inept and clueless certain guys were. Some of us knew how to make beds, but few knew anything about tucking in the bedcovers using hospital corners, so we were all scorned and would soon be paying a price for not knowing how to make a bed in a military fashion. A few days later, we received training on just how footlocker contents and beds should appear. But on that first morning, it was all about ineptness and humiliation.

We were given a few minutes to shower, shave, and hit the head before lining up for the trip to the mess hall. Jaws dropped when trainees first took in the latrine. Shower systems had multiple heads so several guys could shower all at once. Some guys were pretty hesitant about this overt display of male nudity, but most of us could handle it, having experienced something similar in school gyms. What shook many was the array of unscreened toilets set off to one side of the room. Let's just say neither privacy nor modesty were factors. If you were going to do your business, you were going to be on display. End of conversation.

——•——

Everything was "Hurry-up, hurry-up, hurry-up;" the comings and goings were always in "double-time" or "quick-time"—basically a moderate jog.

Except for continually being screamed at and told to rush, however, I enjoyed eating at the mess hall. I worked in restaurants prior to being drafted, felt at home and took it all in. It was fully equipped with familiar stainless-steel fixtures and equipment. It was relatively clean for an old place dropped into what I guessed was previously a World War II-era barracks. But the handful of troops on staff clearly did not want to be there, projecting boredom if not disdain. Still, the whole experience took me out of my thinking and made me want to grab an apron and do something productive and rewarding like cooking and feeding people. It turns out the workers in the Reception Center mess hall were troops assigned to what was called "kitchen police." I soon learned "KP" duty was something of a dreaded rotation assignment that generally lasted twelve hours, from before reveille to after dinner. Unlike most guys, I enjoyed it, although nobody seemed to comprehend why.

After breakfast, our Spec 4 chose some guys to do mundane housekeeping tasks and others to head outside for Butt Patrol—picking up cigarette butts scattered around the barracks and environs. Then he'd disappear for a bit and we'd be left alone to wait. And wait we did for long stretches between meals. We sat on the edges of bunks, paced the barracks, shot the breeze, read, walked outside the immediate area, wrote letters, and tried to come to terms with our situation. This was our first experience of a process the Cadre referred to as "hurry up and wait." You rushed and rushed, and then sat around. This was considered efficient, the standard-operating procedure for doing just about everything. Do what you were told to do fast, then wait around for something foreseeable or unexpected to occur.

At this point we were a ragged bunch of new trainees. Many of us wore long hair, sideburns, beards and/or moustaches. Fatigue shirts were generally not tucked beneath pants, and the pants were not bloused, falling sloppily over dull, high-top leather boots. Caps, when worn, were akimbo. Picture this: hippies in uniform ... Sargent Pepper un-posed and unpretentious.

In some bewildering way you had to love it, even as you hated the idea of everybody walking into this Brave New World of color-coded sameness. The look was "OD," aka "Olive Drab." OD pants, OD shirts, OD tee shirts, OD socks and briefs, OD overcoats, and OD duffle bags. The stuff was made to last, made in America, made for conformity, made to rough-up, made for camouflage. When you wore it, you were informally uniform, even when it got perpetually ruffled. If you liked neutral colors you forgot about what it all stood for and, strange as it seems, you were happy enough. Olive Drab: how might someone describe it? Perhaps a comfortable prison uniform in solitary hue?

With all this time on my hands, I began to contemplate where God was in all this chaos. And if there is divine omnipresence, I wondered *What the heck is God doing here? Right here, among the insults, the putdowns, the humiliation, and the conformity?* Still, I admit to having other overriding secular concerns just then, and this was just the beginning of my military experience. For most of us draftees, our minds were on what was going to happen next. For me though, I wanted to find out to whom I was going to talk about the morality of the war and my reluctant presence in this place.

Tenth

——•——

War Dog

Like a bird on a wire
Like a drunk in a midnight choir
I have tried in my way to be free

Leonard Cohen

After food we were quick-timed over to the barbershop. Here many of us would lose Afros, sideburns, or cascading hippie hair that often flowed down over the neck and shoulders.

We would be shorn for the bargain price of one dollar. No more long hair or nappy heads. Beards, of course, were to be gone; moustaches, too. Through facial gestures and looks, it was clear many of the new troops were quietly livid about this. But they knew there was nothing for it. I have to say a few guys took it in stride and seemed proud to be shorn and shaved, perhaps taking it as a symbol of duty and patriotic status.

I told the barber to just trim my moustache as I saw that some of our Cadre and others had short moustaches that did not go over the lip. He said, "Well that's true, but not for trainees, not in Basic. It all has to come off, even if I have to get someone to hold you down." As he shaved mine, I swore that no matter what the future held no man would ever again be allowed to take it off me so easily. Tough, angry thoughts…but no action from me, at least not that day. Although I could sense I was not alone in feeling humiliated or violated. When Basic ended, I quickly grew the moustache back; and it has never come off since.

———•———

It is true everybody was standing there looking pretty much the same. We were sporting disheveled and rumpled OD fatigues with hair that made us look like we belonged in a monastery. Still looking ragged and akimbo, we were powerless and did not really understand the haircut bought us all down to the same level. The brass called it looking "high and tight." It reminded me of the ubiquitous buzz cut we had all suffered through as boys.

I think it was pretty much agreed by both vendors and customers that those barbers, whoever they were, would not be receiving any tips. Then, latching onto just one of youth's false historical equivalents, my mind drifted to the shorn heads I saw in pictures of POWs and inmates in World War II concentration camps.

After being shorn like sheep, the group was herded outside and ordered to stand "at ease," that is, not ramrod straight like at "attention," but with legs slightly spread, hands clasped behind us in a more relaxed posture. The Commander then addressed us, saying everyone here must complete Basic Training before moving on to advanced training in a particular Military

Occupational Specialty (MOS). Advanced training consisted of any and all military jobs—Infantry, Artillery, Hospital Corp, Mortuary, Cooks and Bakers, Transport, Quartermaster, Clerical, and many, many more. What he did not say was the war was chewing up combat troops by the hundreds; more were needed, especially in Infantry and Artillery.

The Commander said no one would be allowed to fail Basic. One would be tested in accomplishing various feats, like marching or marksmanship. There was to be no such thing as failure in any area, even if it meant doing Basic Training a second time—sort of like summer school for first-time losers. It soon became clear many guys knuckled down and went through the motions just to make sure they did not have to go through this again.

With a knowing nod to the Drill Sergeant, the Commander declared questioning and thinking were not optional. We were not there to think. We did not get paid to think. Thinking was the enemy of this man's army; we do not *think* here, we *do* here.

<hr />

Doing-not-thinking was far more than a way to break the will of trainees and to get everyone to obey orders. Ultimately, it was a technique to get total cooperation in the military, especially in combat situations. The only exception was what they called "thinking with your military mind," a concept also drilled into us. In large measure, this meant constantly being alert or, more immediately, being mindless in favor of obeying commands and taking immediate action.

Doing-not-thinking often turned out to be decent advice. It came in handy over the years when things seemed out of control; for example, when a situation demanded immediate action, like during moments of danger or threat. The idea was to first "do"- and then "think" about it later. I did come to realize there were times when one could not sit there looking very much like the guy in Auguste Rodin's famous statue *The Thinker*. Sometimes there just is no time to ponder or to freeze. There are situations when you only have a split second to react when seeing a person in distress or in real or potential danger. That is when it becomes instinctual and your "military mind" clicks in. Parsing out the correctness of your action and learning from the experience must come later. You go, go, go, head toward the situation, and do, do, do—even when you do not really know what you are doing or the best way to help.

Even if, or perhaps especially when, you are trying to commit to a life of nonviolence.

———•———

Do, do, do! Over the next several months we went over this again and again as we were exposed to new training and experiences. This was my first exposure to the notion of thinking with your military mind—always required in this forsaken place and, for those who listened and learned, later in combat zones. For some of us, sent to combat zones or not, it became part of us. I know it was burned into me. It never went away.

Here's one example where do-don't-think came into play for me during civilian life. A year after I was discharged, I was once again working as a night manager in the fast-food restaurant that held and gave me back my job when I got out of the army. A tile man was replacing the old and difficult-to-clean vinyl flooring with new ceramic tile. The floor was in the back, wrapping around the walk-in refrigerator in the center of the room.

The floor surrounded the refrigerator in something of a square horseshoe. To loosen the vinyl, the tile man poured gasoline on the floor; but he forgot to turn off the water heater.

The natural gas fumes eventually ignited, and the entire back floor leapt into flames. Luckily, the man was by the back door. Screaming "fire" he bolted out. It was late in the afternoon and most of the night shift had yet to arrive for the dinner rush. Fortunately, the few teens with me were in the front cooking or in the customer service areas along with a few customers waiting to be served. I yelled at everyone to "get out!" The customers bolted and workers leapt over the customer service counter and evacuated through the front.

I quickly rolled up the cuffs of my pants, fully revealing my army-issue set of shined but tired black boots. Hey, these were great for ankle support during long shifts on your feet, even if my boss wanted me to get rid of them in favor of black shoes. At this point in my life, I was not taking authority or direction very well.

I ran over to the left side of the walk-in refrigerator, reached around the corner and grabbed the fire extinguisher. Flames were coming up only about six inches, but coats hanging on the wall were beginning to ignite. I moved into the flames spraying fire retardant in front, on the side, and occasionally on patches of fire behind me.

Thankfully, the flames did not come past the tops of my boots! I continued around the horseshoe extinguishing floor and wall, as black smoke began filling the upper portion of the room. I made my way all around until the fire was doused.

Mission accomplished. Parsing it out later, the boss was extremely grateful and I had not gone up in flames. Other than feeling justified for refusing to get rid of my army boots, I can't say I felt much else. That emotional distancing was to continue for decades and took years to even recognize in myself.

I must also admit to some bad decisions, including a couple of split-second hesitations where another stepped in first or I reacted incorrectly. One night, on a poorly lit road, I did not stop driving to check something suspicious out, telling myself I was afraid I would endanger my driving companion. (I still feel guilty about that one.)

Then, there was a robbery involving two bad guys and a gun where my "moving toward the danger" almost got me killed. When the trigger was pulled, the weapon jammed or was empty. I ended up being hit over the head with the pistol: the war dog unleashed, the still incomplete Christian and military-minded Lone Ranger damn near whacked while donning his white hat.

Eleventh

———•——

Fish in a Barrel

I have entered the waters of the deep…
And the waves overwhelm me.

Psalm 69

There are a few books out there that go deeply into the experiences of Basic Training during the Vietnam era. *The Reluctant Lieutenant* by Jerry Morton and *To Benning & Back: The Making of the Citizen Soldier* by Monroe Mann are good resources. The latter takes the form of a diary cataloging daily events in the life of an eager trainee.

But everything you want to know about Basic Training you can learn by watching the feature film *Full Metal Jacket*. Among the raft of excellent Vietnam films, this one and *Gardens of Stone* stand out to me. The former gives a brutally accurate depiction of what it was really like during the early days of military experience; the latter presents an accurate portrayal of dormitory inspections, drill, and the presentation of arms.

In *Full Metal Jacket*, Ronald Lee Ermey, who played the Drill Sergeant, actually was a long time Marine Sergeant before becoming an actor. Nominated for an award for his performance, he was believable *because* he was not acting. *Gardens of Stone* considers the conflicted feelings about the fighting in Vietnam held by military "Lifers" and by new drafted and enlisted personnel. The film depicts a soldier who believes in the correctness of the war, along with those quietly opposed, and the struggles of the conflicted, lifetime Cadre desperate to save the lives of young soldiers.

The word *Cadre* can be broadly defined as a group in military leadership in the U.S. Army. It includes both officers and especially, noncommissioned officers (e.g., soldiers with titles below Second Lieutenant). Officers, of course, make decisions and issue orders; in training units, noncommissioned officers (noncoms) are the every-day face of the unit, carrying out the responsibility of training recruits and conscripts.

———•—

On our first morning of Basic Training, the Monday after the long Fourth of July weekend in 1968, we were awakened by a group of Cadre who came roaring into our dorm. It was absolute chaos. Sleepy, confused guys in their skivvies jumped out of bed. Galvanized trash cans were thrown down the aisle, often with Corporals pounding on the sides of the cans to magnify the din. Screaming and cursing, they rummaged most of our foot and wall lockers we haphazardly put together when on our own over the previous weekend. Personal effects were grabbed and thrown on the bed and floor. Officers were barking out complaints about the way the beds were made. Many ripped the bedding off the springs and tossed it over.

Partially clothed, those of us in training stood awkwardly among the disarray, all the while being screamed at and ridiculed because of the way we looked, who or what we glanced at, and how we answered the Cadre. For the first time, I saw guys systematically roughed up and thrown against bunkbeds and lockers. Meanwhile, there was constant screaming, verbal attacks, and crazy noise coming from all directions. It was pure chaos, terror, and intimidation.

I once heard a troop try to justify this assault as simply "head games," just an initiation, something you had to live through. In his view, the chaos had its purpose. In some small way, the noise and bedlam were meant to mimic the sound and pandemonium of combat. It was a way of shocking us alert; of scaring us into submission. And it worked; we were shocked, and we submitted. We immediately knew exactly who was in charge.

———•———

At some point the chaos stopped and we were ordered to stand in front of the lockers in what was supposed to look like being "at attention." Few of us knew exactly what that really looked like. The instruction was, "Look straight ahead; do not look at anybody's face—especially into our eyes; do not do anything; keep your arms by your side, do not ask questions, just shut up and listen." About mid-room, a crisply dressed fellow wearing a wide-brimmed, so-called "Smokey-the-Bear" hat took over. He was to be our Drill Instructor (DI). He was accompanied by our prim, proper, and extremely imposing Company Commander, a Captain. The Cadre were all nattily dressed fellows in starched pants and khaki shirts. Apparently, this dress was a step up from the green fatigues we had been issued previously. All were perfectly pressed, squared away, and looking "Strack," as we were later trained to say.

These two were accompanied by other men; two of them were the same guys who had been in charge of us over the weekend. These guys continued to prove themselves to be some of the more disagreeable, violent, and possibly psychopathic characters in the human food chain; yet they were Cadre in this training unit. Today, though, they wore a new set of fatigues. Their shirts were tucked-in, their boots were bloused (meaning the cuffs were tucked inside newly shined black boots). I thought to myself, *if only the Drill Sergeant and CO could have seen how disheveled these guys looked over the weekend.* Today they looked like different people, but they were just as ornery, angry, and acerbic to us as they had been before their superiors arrived. They screamed crisply, a viciousness one might equate with authority; this act temporarily masking the total disrespect, disregard, and humiliation behind their words.

Woe to the man who looked into the eyes of the Cadre; they were brow beaten and threatened. Woe to him who could not hold his emotions together or stood there shaking or whimpering; they were punched, pushed, and ridiculed. Perhaps some of us had experienced something similar in a school locker room, during or after a game, but it was all new for most of the men in our ragged group now standing at attention in this old wooden barracks at Fort Dix, New Jersey.

———•———

When things settled down, we were ordered to put fatigues on over our underwear and given less than a minute to comply. Virtually everyone was clamoring to recover clothing from the piles strewn across beds and the floor. Trainees strained to pull together whatever they could in as little time as possible. We were told in short order we must clean-up the disaster *we had created* in the barracks, head outside, and "form-up."

Once outside, we were again reminded we were "maggots," a "gang of worthless, mostly enlistment-dodging, pampered, momma's boys." We were told, "You are here to fight a war, so you better get over all that and get with the program."

Shortly the Drill Instructor, splendid in his wide-brimmed brown hat, joined the Commanding Officer to read us the riot act. We were told to forget both the "subversive hippie counter-culture" with its degenerate and anti-American music, and especially to forget about women. The latter, wives or girlfriends, were sluts anyway (aka, "Suzie Rottencrotch") and were left behind so our draft-dodging friends (aka, "Jody on the block") could screw around with them while we were gone.

We were told the world was a cruel and dangerous place. This camp was a cruel and dangerous place. And we would soon be cruel and dangerous killing machines. That what happens here is what is going to happen, *in spades*, in places like Southeast Asia. They said something like, "Understand this—if you knuckle down here and get lucky you just might come back home in one piece. Then again, you could be brought back as a rotting mass of flesh your family at home, especially Suzie, could not wait to put into the ground. So, get real and get with the program!"

———•———

Now at this point, you might think I am exaggerating or making a lot of this up. Perhaps no other veterans from that era have told you this stuff happened back in those days, and I do not know if these methods were used during training for previous or subsequent wars. I can only hope that training techniques have improved. Maybe many veterans would talk about Basic if they could. Maybe some of them can, but won't. Maybe others won't because, ultimately, they saw much worse. And maybe a lot of them did not make it out of their war alive, something I will grieve forever.

A list of do's and don'ts for us to internalize followed; they were mostly *don'ts*. We were told "Yes, there was a PX on base" where snacks, food, and alcohol were available. But, "No, at this point, maggots could not venture off the grounds to go there." Nor should we treat ourselves to anything resembling soda, candy, or cake; these were said to be off limits during training. It did not matter *how* we got them—at the PX, by mail, or through barter. They were taboo for us the next several weeks. Also, with the exception of wedding rings and wristwatches, no jewelry was allowed.

To further distance ourselves from civilian life, we were told all wristwatches would now be set to 24-hour time. We were no longer to think of time in 1 to 12-hour blocks recurring as AM or PM. From now on 1:00 PM in the afternoon became 13:00 hours, counting up from there until 23:59 (11:59 PM). We were to think this way, talk this way, and calculate time exactly this way and no other way. It sunk in, at least for me. After I was discharged, I kept my watch set to tell time on a 24-hour basis. It remains this way some fifty years later.

Any contraband drugs or alcohol guys snuck in had to be relinquished. Moving forward, none was to be acquired or consumed. Possessing any recreational drugs would get you arrested, probably court-martialed, and sent to the stockade. If any alcohol or snacks were found, the punishment would be swift and severe. You would, "be in a world of hurt," a threat we would hear many times during the next several weeks. Our rigid new Commander made it abundantly clear *he was the guy* in charge. The buck stopped with *him.* To keep an eye on us, a Drill Instructor would be sleeping in the bedroom at the end of the barracks. Additional DIs were to be assigned to the other barracks. All DIs were to be obeyed completely, no matter *how they acted* or *what they told us to do.* No questions and no exceptions allowed. Period.

We would run two miles every day before heading to the mess hall and double-time it the rest of the time. Today, though, we would head straight to the mess hall and then begin training immediately. For now, we were quickly instructed how to march by stepping off with our left foot, then the right, following the cadence, "Your left, your left, your left, right, left." Legs and arms akimbo, we all "marched" over to the mess hall for chow.

Once outside the mess hall, we lined up in single file. To enter, we first had to navigate the dozen or so parallel bars just outside the door. Under the eyes of various Cadre, most guys proved unable to do it. Berated and humiliated, they were sent to the end of the line to try again. Since the Cadre ate after the troops, that punishment did not last too long—the first couple weeks at best. Soon it would be humiliation and "dropping" for push-ups; as in "Give me 10!" Or more. Meanwhile, during the constant screaming, some guys learned to traverse the bars, but most were able to do only two or three before giving up and dropping off. At best, guys would do a few, drop, walk a step or two, get yelled at, do a few more, drop again, and then run in. Later, when only one DI was watching, it was easy to cause a distraction in the line during times when the more hopeless cases were trying to fake their way through.

Once inside, the line was instructed to approach the stainless-steel serving section where sleep-deprived guys on Kitchen Police duty would dish out food. We could choose whatever we wanted but must eat it all (shades of childhood days when the nuns instructed us not to waste food; that when eating we must remember "the starving children of China.") I now thought of the starving war-torn children of Vietnam. So, okay, there would be no leftovers allowed in this mess hall. Often, with few choices, I learned to eat many things I previously avoided. Thank God for Louisiana Red's Hot Sauce.

We were given a short time to eat, short enough to force guys to gobble down food. At the table, we were not allowed to sit properly in our chairs. We were ordered to sit only on the front edge of the chair. Guys who inadvertently slid onto a chair were screamed at and were often knocked over; both troops and utensils crashing to the floor.

The Cadre did ease up on this after a few weeks. Still, the average guy would trip up in many small ways in the weeks to come, suffering the berating, punishments, and humiliations that came with it—even the guys who seemed to want to be there. The latter included a few older guys who had previously been in another branch of the military. For one reason or another they wanted back in, doing something different. Some expressed a dislike for their earlier experience in the navy or air force. Some missed being deployed oversees for what they called, "Fun, Travel and Adventure." So, they re-enlisted into the army, willing to suffer through Basic again as a way to their goal. Others were in Basic as a steppingstone to other training. If they were going to be in, they wanted to do it as officers, so they hoped to attend Officer's Candidate School (OCS). Other willing enlistees saw Basic as a necessary initiation toward their promised goal of going into non-combat training and jobs. Or so they were promised by their recruiters. What they did not realize was those "promises" meant nothing to their new handlers. Some would be sent to the training they signed-up for; many were simply lied to by recruiters or their expressed preference for a specific job was just ignored as they found themselves ordered to Advanced Infantry Training or sent into the Artillery.

For now, we were all just maggots; lost boys trapped in the now known lost cause called Vietnam. Maggots. Eunuchs for the kingdom of pain.

Twelfth

— •◦• —

Visitation

I turned every way, but there was no one to help me.
I looked for one to sustain me, but I could find no one.

Isaiah 63:5

During one formation in Basic, we were told it would be possible to speak with the Company Commander (CO). The door was open and you just had to put in a request to see him. We were told guys went to the Company Commander for any number of reasons. Perhaps they had a serious hardship at home and felt a need to return. Some enlistees needed to be reassured they would be sent to learn a particular Military Occupational Specialty (MOS) and wanted to make sure this was actually going to happen. Some, like me, had been drafted and, for any number of reasons, did not think they belonged and were drafted against their will. It was a relief to know such an option was available. I considered it a key opportunity to talk about my situation and my feelings concerning the war.

Lots of guys were expressing serious concerns about being part of a military force fighting the unpopular war in Vietnam. Absolutely none of us knew a soldier could apply for conscientious objector status after being inducted, and we were certainly never told about it once we took the oath. Nevertheless, there were untold numbers of young men who were opposed to the war and killing. Apparently, there were even more who could accept being there but wanted a MOS where picking up a weapon would be unlikely. I met a number of these men—more and more—as we fraternized with one another.

The Sergeant's spiel about meeting the Company Commander was pro forma, something the Cadre had to cover. One was probably never supposed to take them up on the offer, but I did. After that formation, I told my Drill Sergeant I wanted to see the CO. I could see from his facial expression that he thought I was a damn fool.

In a day or so, I was removed from formation and told to go over to the Orderly Room. There in a sparse, tidy office sat the Company Commander and a lower-level officer I was told would take notes. The latter was really documenting statements and events, and if needed would serve as a witness in the future. What did I know? I thought he was a trainee or something, somebody aspiring to a higher rank and was learning the ropes or being mentored.

I saluted and stood at attention until being told to have a seat. I told them the whole story, how I got here, and why I should not be here. The CO, sharply dressed yet this time comfortably wrinkled, listened with divided attention while signing papers and shuffling things around. I saw a glint of recognition when I mentioned being a Catholic. He even looked up as I expressed my concerns about the contradictions between my religious upbringing and what I might be ordered to do in the future. I suggested some of the things we were to learn might not fit in with the messages received in my faith tradition.

The Company Commander then pointed out the obvious, saying his records did not indicate I came into the army as a noncombatant conscientious objector. I told him I had been fully aware it was possible to apply for this option through the Selective Service System, but even though I had previously gotten the conscientious objection application from my draft board I had chosen not to apply. Neither the Selective Service System nor the U.S. Army recognized selective objection to a particular war; one had to be opposed to all wars. Still, I argued, I did oppose the Vietnam War and should be administratively discharged.

—•—

It was quite clear the CO had heard enough. He took control of the interview by saying, "I see you have two years of college, trainee. That doesn't make you an intellectual." Continuing, he pointed out I was not alone in coming to see him. Lots of troops, especially draftees, felt they did not belong here. He then said something close to the following, "At some point most GIs think they are in the wrong place." He continued, "Any number of guys come to see me, especially after we visit the rifle range. They all say they aren't suited for this; they don't want to do this. They, too, want out of the army. You are no different."

He then proudly proclaimed, "I've been to Vietnam. I did my duty. I understand the country is split over the issue, so I'm not surprised guys like you end up here feeling the same way.

But the reality is, you were drafted; you are here now. Maybe you don't belong in one of the combat arms, but you will be in Basic Training for the next several weeks."

He argued besides military training we would be learning many things useful in civilian life. He said we should pay attention to every situation and make the best of what we were about to experience; and in addition to all the training we were getting physically fit—many for the first time in our young lives. He mused some guys knew very little about living, even how to make their beds. He referred to a film we recently watched showing guys how to brush their teeth, suggesting a number of these guys came right out of the sticks and had no idea how to even do this correctly. Underscoring the point, he mused, "Hell, it cost this army big money to put teeth in your mouths and provide you with glasses. We want you to learn to take care of yourselves; so there are plenty of useful things you can learn." He continued, "Is there harsh discipline? Yeah. There's nothing wrong with having discipline. We have to have it here. You will need discipline on your jobs and in other areas of your life. Just make the best of what you learn here. Try to use it to your advantage."

———•———

He then laid down the law by reaffirming something I already knew: "You know the drill; if you are away from your duty station or absent for more than twenty-four hours you will be subject to the charge of being Absent Without Leave (AWOL). If you are gone longer than thirty days, we might charge you with desertion. We turn the information over to the Feds. They *will* find you, detain you, and whisk you off to one of our bases.

Eventually we will court-martial you. When you lose your case, you will be going back to the stockade. If you are constantly uncooperative you may be sentenced to Fort Leavenworth prison for disobeying orders and you will get a dishonorable discharge."

He finished up saying his hands were tied. He declared the ball was now in my court saying, "So you see, it's up to you, Private, to make a decision. You have to look at reality. We are here now, some of us by choice, others not so much. But my job is this: I've got to get you through Basic. Let's see how it goes. I certainly will note this in your file along with my advice, which is just this: that you stay, that you go through the motions and pass all your tests. Maybe the results will indicate you should be a clerk or something. For now, it behooves you to get with the program and stay out of trouble. Then, if you still feel the same way when you move on to your next duty station you can bring up your concerns with them."

Once again, I heard the familiar excuse many before him thought might change my mind. He said, "Look, there are plenty of ways a guy with a good education can be used in a manner where both the army and you can be happy." He finished up abruptly, saying he appreciated me coming to see him and to remember I could always come back if I had additional concerns. Just like that, we were done. I saluted the CO where he sat, did something resembling an about face, and left.

———•———

I walked out of there upset and frustrated. As a civilian I had been up against the full power of the U.S. government embodied in the rules and regulations of the Selective Service System.

Now I found myself up against the full force of the U.S. Army, considered the most powerful military in the world. Nobody was listening. Nobody cared as long as a nobody, like me, threw a wrench into their well-oiled machines. Again, the questions consumed me. What was the right thing to do? Trusting and naïve, I did not fully realize it was all a game, a way for the system—the factotums at Selective Service and our Company Commander—to pretend to be understanding while actually being condescending and threatening. Months later, I saw no notes about this meeting appearing in my file. Nor were there any in the Military Intelligence or FBI files I got some twenty years later after using the Freedom of Information Act.

Officially, this meeting never happened.

Thirteen

—— • ——

Strack Troop

You may choose whether or not to fight,
but once fighting, your power of choice is gone.

Gilbert Murray

One of the Cadre's main goals during Basic Training was to turn our ragged group of disparate individuals into a highly trained, cohesive military force. The metamorphosis included the troops becoming something resembling the way *they* were. That is, we were to become "Strack Troops" and "Lean Mean Killin' Machines." To be Strack one had to meet certain conditions; for example, the brass insignia worn on one's Dress Green uniform had to be thoroughly shined, looking pristine. To do this properly you needed to acquire Brasso metal polish, an amazingly effective solvent that cleaned up buckles and brass insignia no matter how tarnished they became.

Your attire was expected to feature sharp creases starched into dress clothes and even into the fatigues we wore daily. The latter was essentially impossible for the average trainee, given the demands of physical training, marching, and maneuvers. You were simply not able to keep the dirt off fatigues during Basic and Advanced Infantry Training (AIT); forget about keeping them starched.

I do not remember any trainee ironing fatigues. In fact, I don't recall ever using an iron. If you're Cadre, or doing a routine army job, you sent them out to the base laundry. I do not think that option was available to us, so our fatigues were pretty much demolished by midweek. Washing them on Sunday afternoon became essential.

Then there were guys like me who, although it was summer, slept in their fatigue bottoms—if not in both bottoms and tops. Doing so saved precious seconds when you were aroused in the middle of the night for formations and/or by a Cadre intent on keeping you constantly alert. So, half-asleep and always exhausted, you slept in your fatigues. This way all you had to do amid the screaming and demands to "Hurry, hurry, hurry!" was to pull on your boots.

Frankly, although I worked hard to keep them clean, I really did not care how my fatigues looked; like others, I paid minimal concern to this protocol. I got the sense most Cadre also felt this way. The only time wrinkled fatigues became an issue was when some troop screwed up in another area or especially during unannounced barracks inspections.

But you know what? Those OD fatigues still had many benefits, despite their dour similarity and the challenge of keeping them clean and pressed. They were cotton, they were loose, there were plenty of pockets, and to my surprise I took a liking to them.

One of the more helpful ideas for being Strack involved using Five-Day Deodorant Pads. These, of course, were totally useless on filthy, smelly bodies. However, they were great for spit-shining your boots and shoes. Guys were under pressure to keep boots cleaned and shined, despite our dusty, muddy training environments. Five-Day Deodorant Pads put a fierce shine on your otherwise scuffed and ratty boots or shoes. Footwear was always supposed to be highly polished, especially when stored in wall lockers, in formations, and during inspections or travel. One of the guys previously in another branch of the military brought some with him and alerted us to its usefulness, and it spread like wildfire, especially once we were allowed to go to the PX for supplies.

Of course, given the demands of training, it all seemed incredibly absurd. Joking around, one guy suggested, "Hey, if things get really tough when we go home back to the World, we can always shine shoes for a living. What the heck, it beats selling pencils!" Truth be told, any one of us could end up doing this—and we knew it. Little did we know just how bad the future would get for some struggling Vietnam veterans.

Some twenty years later in New York City, and in many other urban centers, about twenty-five percent of the homeless population were estimated to be veterans. A new generation of homeless veterans had joined the dwindling ranks of marginalized World War II vets. With sleeping bags and cardboard boxes, they too now lived on the streets. One day, while walking with my wife in Manhattan, a middle-aged guy with a shoe-shine box yelled out to us, "Your lady looks fine, but your shoes need a shine!" We looked at each other and laughed, even as visions of deodorant pads and the dark humor of my barracks-mate immediately came flooding in.

We were constantly reminded by the Cadre that being Strack also meant definitely not smiling during formation or looking officers in the eye, especially when being inspected or dressed down.

———•———

Stripes indicated one's level of rank. Three stripes or more equaled being a Sergeant. No matter how many stripes they had, however, Drill Sergeants were not to be called "Sergeant," but "Drill Sergeant." There were many different levels or ranks of Sergeants, along with some Corporals, and others up the chain, who wore "Specialist" insignia. We needed to learn them all, including the metal insignia worn by the officers. Those with a diamond in the middle were First Sergeants. Some people were permitted to call him "Top," as in "Top Sergeant" or "Top Dog." Of course, maggots such as ourselves were not permitted to use these informal nicknames.

In all cases, you never called any type of Corporal or Sergeant, "Sir." That designation was used only for officers. This we learned early on after some poor soul being browbeaten barked, "No Sir!" to a Sergeant. The response was immediate, typically abusive, and included the memorable phrase, "Don't call me 'Sir!' I work for a living."

This was a profound statement, one rich with truth. In fact, the Sergeants truly did run everything. They essentially ran the trainee operation, the mess halls, the quartermaster operations, the orderly room, and more. Sure, the buck stopped with the officers and the latter could dictate commands coming from above—but they were just as likely to stand down and take the advice of the Sergeants when it came to operations. It was the non-commissioned officers (non-coms) who got things done.

For many of these guys, the army was a career and they were proud of it. Generically, they were called "Lifers" because they were in it for the long haul. They believed in their work. They showed up every day and accomplished their missions. They solved problems, got things done, worked with and cajoled officers, and mentored the troops. In the army, I learned something from non-coms about middle-management: working for the people, working with and around the power structure, staying the course, keeping one's eye on the prize. These folks truly "worked for a living," a phrase I later found applicable to those of us in civilian middle-management, who despite the designs of our superiors are generally the ones who get things done in most organizations.

Being Strack also meant standing correctly in formation, at parade rest, when handling a weapon in a certain way; and always walking straight and crisply. If you were an officer or a noncommissioned officer, walking also seemed to include the right to swagger.

No umbrellas were allowed. Well, we were not this, that, or the other thing associated with being female in this man's army. When walking you also looked straight ahead, you did not "bop around" like some "Jody on the block." The Cadre snickered as they suggested "Jody" was too busy to "bop" anyway, due to "servicing" your girlfriend or wife while you were away. "You copy that, troop?"

As time went on the Cadre and less frequently the Commanding Officer would stride through for a spot inspection. When they came through, you had to hope your boots were perfectly shined, your brass gleamed, your footlocker and wall locker were organized, and your duffel bag was neatly appointed. They would come through, occasionally jaw at one of the troops for some sort of minor infraction—usually demanding ten, twenty, or more push-ups as a punishment for whatever shortcoming they discovered. The random browbeating, cursing, name-calling, you name it continued, directed toward any one of the troops.

When they checked me out one time, I knew I had my act together. Boots shined? Indeed. Brass polished? Check. Toiletries perfectly placed in my footlocker? Got that. Wall locker squared-away? Oh yeah.

Out of nowhere our Commanding Officer notices a protrusion visible from the side of the duffel bag hanging on my wall locker. True, it was not completely smooth and pear shaped, but it was cleanly packed; yet something in it was getting his attention. He rips the bag off the locker, slams it down on the bed, reaches in and pulls out a pile of letters and cards received from family and friends. Now I think it is fair to ask why someone would hold onto such stuff once the correspondence was read and answered. I guess I was just missing home and being nostalgic. Otherwise, I really did not have a reason to keep them. But still, among all the mad minutes we were experiencing, they did bring me peace and give me a connection to home. Innocent enough, I thought.

But not in the eyes of our demanding Company Commander. He gets into my face and starts humiliating me, questioning my manhood, calling me all sorts of misogynistic names. For all to hear, he mocks my behavior, cooing, "Ahh, isn't this cute?" He throws the cards all over the bed and joined his minions who stood there smiling, indeed laughing, basking in the experience of watching a powerless maggot being belittled.

I was smart enough to understand this performance was just another example of breaking people down by humiliating them. But this time it was personal; and I was livid. My mind raced: Of all the things that made an impression on him, of all the things done right, of all the personal compromises made in attempts to cooperate, of all the things that had been taken from me—taken from all of us—this, this connection to the outside and the people I loved, belonged to *me*. And he was brutal. He did not rip stuff up, but he told the group I was a "wimp" and ordered me to, "Clean that pathetic mess up," as he moved on to inspect his next victim.

I stood there seething; feeling misused, trapped, and overwhelmed, wanting vengeance. I saw this as an attack, not only on me but by extension on my family; on "La Familia." At that moment, I joined so many others in my generation who no longer trusted authority; those who ascribed to the then currently popular dictum, "Don't trust anyone over 30." In the minds of some of us in the Vietnam generation, this also meant it was unwise to trust anyone, regardless of age, who wore metal insignia, anyone from young Lieutenants on up. It was a class distinction. They were the elites. We were "maggots," "GIs" ("Government Issues"), replaceable parts, categorizations continually reinforced and never to be forgotten. On this day, the CO and his subordinates succeeded in getting me truly angry. I was livid. Apparently, the training was meant to unleash a maggot's inner anger, i.e., awaken a rage that could eventually be directed toward a foreign enemy. It was beginning to work.

The Cadre referred to protocol as doing things the "Army Way," and "getting with the program." One either complied or found himself doing push-ups or being severely reprimanded. One punishment we found extremely humiliating and obnoxious was being ordered to assume the so-called "Dying Cockroach Position."

There was even a Strack way of taking the dying cockroach position. Guys were supposed to get on their backs and hold both arms and legs up as if one were vermin taking its last breath. After the first time I saw this, I refused to watch. I always looked away, seething, when some poor guy was punished this way. Many of us empathized with him, feeling just as embarrassed and humiliated as he obviously did. At any time, we knew this could happen to anyone; secretly we hoped it did not happen to us. The first time I saw this particular kind of humiliation, I told myself I would refuse to do it. To comply or not comply? Once again, that was the question. Do you risk a violent reaction…or even the stockade? Or do you swallow your pride and get with the program? Some eager recruits willingly assumed the position. Most of us watched in communal humiliation and fear. I never saw anybody refuse, and luckily I was never ordered to assume the position. In this case, at least, I did not have to test my resolve.

That particular punishment was bad enough, but in my mind there was something even more degrading that came our way—something even worse than this immediate and the off-the-cuff punishment dealt out for the slightest offence. I cannot recall its official name, but it was essentially being ordered to crawl like a snake for great distances. I'll call it the "snake-walk."

It is embarrassing for me to tell this story, and many times I thought about leaving it out of this book. However, one main reason I am writing it is to let those who are thinking about joining the military know what some of us encountered, and what they perhaps still might experience. This may be especially helpful for those with doubts about enlisting and for those recruits who come to question what they are seeing and doing. I can only hope training in the U.S. military has changed for the better and that punishments like this are no longer used. Enlistees should be treated with respect, though I doubt they are, even now.

So, with great trepidation, and no small amount of lingering anger and deep embarrassment bordering on pain, I must relate this tale. Some weeks into Basic Training, following a training exercise or rifle range session, we were told to hurry to retrieve our gear and saddle up. As usual, the command was to snap it on quickly before being called to attention. The last guy caught getting this done would be "one sorry-assed troop." That day, to my great surprise and total disbelief, that person was me.

I'm sure this was not the first time I was one of the last to complete something, but this time I was the one who got caught. The guy who spotted me was now crazy-mad and demanding retribution. Worse, this time I was caught by one of those sociopathic corporals we met the first night we arrived at Basic Training.

Our group was about to head to a mess hall that stood about a football field away. Screaming, threatening, and generally in-my-face, the corporal ordered me to get on the ground and crawl back to the mess hall. Just a few days earlier, I watched this same corporal take his helmet—his "Steel Pot"—and hit a trainee so hard from behind that the guy fell face forward onto the ground. This corporal was one mean dude, and all the guys tried not to upset him; he was one guy I did not want to mess with, at all.

In a heartbeat all the socialization from parents and teachers set in, the instruction, the admonitions, the warnings, the negative experiences associated with going your own way, the consequences, the pain. "Don't think, do" was taking over, but I *was* thinking, even if I did not know it:

"Obey those in authority…"
"Go along, get along…"
"Don't rock the boat, don't make waves…"
"Don't be seen as a troublemaker…"
"Stay out of trouble..."
"Use common sense, Jerry."

But I was trapped, and my reaction was to cop an immediate attitude. Angry, exhausted and not thinking clearly, I thought, *I'll show him!*

Down I went. I hit the ground. My first thought was *so much for having a Strack-looking uniform.* I began the snake-walk, slithering along; one of the maggots we were said to be. Crawling face first in the dirt, like during training when snaking underneath barbed wire, supposedly with live machine-gun rounds blasting over our heads.

Angry and aching I kept crawling, determined to make it to the mess line to join my company. *I'll show him. I'll show him, that SOB.* Meanwhile, the rest of my company had double-timed over to the mess hall and were now falling into formation.

I had gone several yards when my tormentor decided he had enough. He was probably as tired as the rest of us and just wanted the day to end. For whatever reason, he told me to get up and run to the mess hall, all the while using terminology that should not be repeated. I told him to forget about it, that I was under orders. Blowing him off, I kept crawling. At that point, he kicked me in the ribs and ordered me to get up and get the hell out of there. As if looking for understanding, he screamed he was hungry and I was keeping him from sitting down to eat. I wanted to jump up and hit him. But now, having been physically attacked, I recalled the violent nature of the guy I was messing with; I got up glaring and painfully jogged back to my company.

I was beyond anger. Indeed, I soon came to fully understand I was in a very violent place—the dark, non-thinking hellhole of vengeance, rage, and action they wanted me to reach. Unconsciously, I looked for some way to strike back.

When forced to snake-walk, you were expected to fall-in at the back of the line. It was as simple as that. Today I was the last person to comply with the directive so, I would also be the last troop to eat. Livid, tired, embarrassed, filthy, and hungry, I needed an outlet. I needed that more than I needed food; I needed to break something, to blow something up, to cause pain. I soon found it. Instead of stopping at the end of the line, which was composed of several different units, I went up to join my unit at the back of their line.

The first guy in the line immediately behind my unit stood about 6'3" tall, as compared to my 5'10". He could tell from my appearance I was the snake walker. He demanded to know what I was doing, cutting in. I told him I was linking up with my unit, and in solidarity with them I was joining them at the back of their line. With a shove he yelled, "The hell you are!" pushing me off the queue. At this point everything that happened previously came to a head—the grueling training, the exhaustion, the loss of dignity, the humiliation of not living up to my resolve. I was a pressure cooker with a lid now ready to explode.

Quickly my Christian training about turning the other cheek was ignored. In a heartbeat and a red-hot "Do, don't think" moment, I hammered this guy a couple of quick times. He stumbled over a railroad tie and went down on one knee.

Suddenly, I came to realize what I had done. I saw him charging toward me arms and fists flailing, ready to beat the living hell out of me. I covered my face like a boxer and absorbed the blows until a Drill Sergeant ran over and tore us apart. He ordered us both to back down; saying this animosity between us was not to continue. He said we would settle this issue in the future in a boxing ring with gloves or pugil sticks. (That never happened.) The DI left me where I stood. The big guy was banished to the end of his unit's line, giving us enough space to cool off. I don't remember ever crossing paths with him again.

<figure>—•—</figure>

Over the next few days, I replayed the episode in my head, trying to make sense of what had happened and how I had reacted. *"Why did you originally cave-in and go along with the punishment? What, you didn't want to make a show before the rest of the group? What would have happened if you did? Would that sadistic Corporal have knocked you down in front of everyone? Would the officers just scream and berate me, hauling me off to the orderly room for a good dressing down? Would they call the MPs and have me taken to the stockade? Why did you refuse to cooperate later, when you were alone with that maniac, knowing full well what he was capable of?"* And, most disturbing and complex, I pondered *"Why did you take out your anger on your fellow innocent, albeit obnoxious, troop?"*

I decided my violent reaction was exactly what I was being trained to do. Anger, vengeance, and retaliation was part of the program being developed here. I had fallen into the trap and succumbed to it. I let this idea seep into me. I had no clue how I would handle the humiliations and moral conundrums that surely lie ahead; for now, I told myself I would not let my anger get the best of me again.

Of course, it did. Sins continually forgiven…shame eternally borne. *Mea culpa, mea culpa, mea maxima culpa.*

Fourteenth

Firing Line

Develop in every soldier during training
the confidence, will, knowledge, and skills
required to fire a rifle and hit enemy personnel in combat.

U.S. Army Field Manual (FM) 23-8

On the day we were issued our M-14s, we were introduced to the memorable and dramatic rallying cry, "This is my rifle! This is my gun! One is for killing, the other for fun!" We were to memorize it and would repeat it over and over moving forward. At first when screaming this mantra, we were ordered to hold the weapon up and yell, "This is my rifle!" Then, pointing to our crotches, to shriek, "This is my gun!" We finished the final sentence with the roar, "One is for killing, the other for fun!" The first statement taught us to never use the word *gun* but rather *rifle* or *weapon.* The second suggested comic relief, but it also linked love and lust to power and death. Overall, the mantra connected sex to killing. We were to channel our sexuality into violence.

We were also told the empty rifle issued to us was our friend. When it was loaded, it was our best friend. In time, it would come with us most everywhere. We would train with it, march with it, and learn to fire and clean it. We were never to let it out of our sight, both here and on training maneuvers. If we went on bivouac, we slept with it.

We learned to properly carry them: handling them in formation, while standing at parade rest, and during inspections. We picked them up from a caged shed, stacked them tee-pee style between training exercises, and returned them to the shed at the end of the day. We learned to move crisply and fluidly, presenting arms using detailed choreography. When standing at parade rest, the rifles functioned like a crutch, a third leg; so, more than one exhausted guy fell asleep while standing. I was one of those guys. Twice.

—•—

The M-14, 7.62mm rifle was standard issue at the time in Basic Training at Fort Dix, slowly being replaced with the lighter, more agile M-16; the latter now used in Advanced Infantry Training and being introduced into Vietnam. The M-14 was heavy, weighing about ten pounds, a bit more when loaded.

We learned how to break it down, how to oil and clean it, how to load and unload empty clips of ammunition, and told we would soon be locking and loading live rounds. When I held it, I noticed it had an eerily familiar feel to it—something like a baseball bat, sure; but pointedly more primordial—a club, spear, or sword perhaps—as if I once carried something lethal before. Perhaps some distant ancestors of mine did. More likely those humble Italian sharecroppers simply carried a hoe, plunging it into the living earth of some fruitful Sicilian farm.

Then too, the *click* sound of loading a magazine, though new, was also oddly enthralling. Click. It's loaded. Click. It's ready. Click. Time to rock n' roll. Strangely drawn to it, I have never forgotten the sound or feel. Even now when I click a battery into a power tool, I flash back to that time. Click. I'm ready to rock n' roll. Go figure.

Our M-14 was an automatic, able to fire twenty rounds at a time. However, I cannot recall shooting in automatic mode. We did fill the cartridge magazines, but we were either ordered to switch to semi-automatic or were not allowed to fire it with the selector switched to automatic.

One morning we boarded trucks and were driven to the firing range. The Sergeant on duty gave a lecture on how to conduct ourselves while at the range. He reaffirmed how to carry weapons whether empty or loaded, especially when loaded. He demonstrated various positions, standing and firing from the shoulder, while kneeling, and while lying down. We would practice each of these as a range instructor came by and adjusted postures. We went there frequently in the weeks that followed, being tested on accuracy from time to time.

As we settled in on the firing line, I noticed two things. The first was a small, but not insignificant number of guys who were teary eyed or actually sobbing; firing rifles was not something they wanted to do, whatever their reasons. Second, I noted the presence of a few chaplains on the grounds. These officers were not only there to observe, but to support the proceedings; to bless what we were doing, as it were.

The range instructor directed them to head over to the guys who were breaking down. Their job was to reassure these guys everything was okay. They visited each man, gave an encouraging pat, wiped a tear from a cheek, and probably gave assurance God was on our side. Not one of these troops was ever escorted off the range. The comforting words streamed from the lips of those clerics who simultaneously lived the paradox of rendering to Caesar and giving to God. For them, killing for one's country was not murder. Somehow, they saw little difference between what the troops were doing and the words of love they preached and supposedly modeled. Their presence and message contradicted much of what many of us previously learned at church, school, and home.

I was disappointed and disgusted, their expressions of loving-kindness aside; I was appalled by the absence of any moral leadership or authority, of speaking to the truth, of addressing notions of good and evil. My opinion of chaplains began to change that day, even as I appreciated the comfort provided to those who were in distress. I empathized with those guys thinking, "Be strong brothers, I should not be doing this either. None of us should."

Still, I never lost complete faith in the chaplains, although on a personal level I was let down by them again and again. Then, as now, I recognized the aching need for spiritual services and the help and guidance always needed on a military base. That day, I developed a critical eye that began slowly eating away at my unquestioned respect for the clergy. For the first time I saw the chaplains, the "men of God," as human beings, some holier than others, some not holy at all.

Later one fellow rationalized it this way, "Hey, they're officers too, what do you expect?" I was not alone in wishing they were either civilians assigned to the base or, at best, non-commissioned officers—Sergeants or Specialists. Something closer to what the average troop was or hoped to be. Someone to help differentiate the sacred from the secular. I think I would have been able to identify with them more; I was not alone feeling this way.

—•—

While waiting for the chaplains to clear the firing range, I remembered the fruitless talk I had with our Company Commander. He had suggested I take advantage of various military things that came my way during training. Naïvely, I decided one way to do this was to *absolutely* eat up as much ammunition as possible. Foolishly, I reasoned this would prove to be quite expensive for the army. Indeed, the Cadre always made a point of telling us the cost of individual rounds, grenades, and equipment we were to use. My naive young mind concluded every bullet fired into a paper target, or by purposely wasting a shot, meant one less bullet that might go into a human being somewhere in Southeast Asia.

With this in mind, I was more than ready to fire that weapon. Soon the instructor barked out the safety command, "Ready on the left; ready on the right! Ready on the firing line!" When all was set and the area cleared, he screamed, "Fire!" So, I fired, and I fired, and I fired. Round after round; clip after clip. Day after day. Bam, Bam, Bam. Squeeze the trigger. Waste those rounds. Destroy that ammunition.

Immature, crazy thinking to be sure, and totally ineffective when it came to wasting money and resources. Still, I'm glad I did it, and I'll never forget the raw power in the firing stick I was holding; before this I thought using a baseball bat made you feel your power. This was something else, quite simply it was the power over life and death.

Eventually, they announced I was a "Marksman." I had accomplished the objectives listed in *FM 23-8*. I had acquired the "confidence" to handle weapons; I had the "knowledge" to maintain and utilize them; and I possessed the "skill" needed to accurately fire them. But ignored by the brass, I did not have the "will" to "hit enemy personnel." In and of itself, shooting weapons did not change my negative feelings about the war. Nor did it increase my desire to hunt men or animals.

Just about every troop loved to shoot. We were kids. What boy did not like the pure power of firing weapons, of blowing things up? In their earlier lives, some guys had experienced hunting; like me, many had used illicit fireworks. The power and thrill of it was all too familiar. At this point, most of us were unable to imagine what the Cadre who were training us had already seen. From experience, most of them knew exactly what those weapons could do and what those explosions meant. As our experience grew and a few members of Cadre shared their stories, we would learn much more of this. But at this point, perhaps we were too power drunk, too confused, too submissive, or too deep in mass denial. In any case, although we had learned much, we understood little.

And it was already too late.

Fifteenth

——▶●◀——

Spirit of the Bayonet

So that with much ado I was corrupted;
and made to learn the dirty devices of this world.

Rev. Thomas Traherne

Call: "What's the Spirit of the Bayonet!?"
Response: "To kill!"
Call: "I can't hear you!"
Response: "To kill!"
Call: "Sound off like you gotta' pair!"
Response: "To kill!"

The shrieked ferocity of this mantra went on for several minutes. At first, I did not respond, as much in shock as in stunned amazement. Then I noticed several guys were replacing "kill" with sexually explicit expletives. Humored and enthused, I joined in. Of course, our personal protests were drowned out by the massive din of the excited troops; still, it felt good to appear to cooperate while making a mockery of their attempts to indoctrinate us. Over time, we heard different variations of this cry; perhaps the most obnoxious response being: "To kill men, women, and children, Sergeant/Sir!"

Bayonet training meant learning how to quickly lock the M-6 bayonet onto the end of our M-14 rifles. It was used in close combat or in more traditional assaults, which we were advised just did not happen in Vietnam. One instructor mused, "Hell, we don't do large assaults against positions anymore, we just light 'em up. We turn the place into dust and rubble, bodies into torn flesh and a bloody pink-haze." American firepower thrown at an enemy was immense, he explained. Of course, these days even our small arms were particularly accurate and covered long distances—destructive and deadly in and of themselves.

———•———

Bayonet instruction included how to correctly hold the rifle, how to move forward, and where and how to bury the bayonet into your opponent's body. The most appropriate insertion point was similar to what we were taught about using KA-bar knives, that is, to plunge it into the "V" just below the rib cage. When using either weapon, we should attempt to push up, not straight through, thereby inflicting maximum damage by twisting and tearing up the organs.

Both types of blades had a "blood groove" on one side. This allowed you to pierce an opponent, easily draw it out, and then deliver the coup de grace. Custom-made for rapid use in close, hand-to-hand combat.

Previously, on the firing line I saw some troops who did not want to shoot a weapon, no less learn how to use it to shoot someone else. Today, some guys balked at being involved in bayonet training. They certainly did not want to run somebody through with a blade. Once again, I noticed if brow beating, personal assaults against masculinity, or outright threats of punishment did not force cooperation in this training, the chaplains were called to coax those lost lambs gently back to the imagined slaughter.

I thought to myself; *What did those chaplains say? Did they reference Longinus the Centurion, the soldier who plunged his spear into the side of Christ, the storied first military recruit to Christianity? Did they emphasize his militarism while ignoring his second thoughts and conversion?* Soldier to Christian. Christian to soldier. This was us.

We formed into four single ranks to execute the motions, one group at a time per rank. On command we were ordered to scream, "Kill!" as we charged, thrusting at human shaped dummies or at plastic bags filled with hay. Most of these were outfitted in a North Vietnam Army cap or helmet or in a Viet-Cong black shirt. Many of us shouted obscenities as we went through the motions…afraid of punishment, distrustful of the chaplains…we comprised the defiant confederacy of the forsaken. The screaming sons of Abraham, rejecting authority and desperate to get off the pyre.

——•——

Once again, I went through the movements. To the Cadre, I was now proficient in staying alive during another potentially frightful and extraordinary catastrophe. But what was my personal take-away? What was applicable to everyday military, civilian, or spiritual life? What in God's name did I just reluctantly, but actually, do? No, I did not revert to or discover some primordial, instinctive, frenzied blood lust. No, I was just disgusted—with myself, with those who led us, with the chaplains—with the whole bloody mess. No, I was not changed. Hell no, I still rejected the war.

When bayonet drill was over, we stacked our rifles and headed off for another class. I could see many of us were mortified, embarrassed, afraid, or just plain grateful this was over. Nobody said a word. Not once did I hear anybody talk or boast about this experience. If you have ever wondered why veterans of combat rarely tell their stories, start by attempting to understand the place where trainees go from innocence to immersion.

Sixteenth

Situation Normal All Fouled Up

> Let no one seek to know from me
> what I know that I do not know.
>
> Augustine of Hippo

SNAFU, that's what we learned to call any number of screw-ups and downright gaffes made by someone in the chain of command, such as operations getting bogged down by paper-work or personnel not following through efficiently. One common example, a request may have been made for trucks to pick us up somewhere, but for some reason they did not arrive or showed up much later than expected. We were always made to hurry to go somewhere, but all too often we would just sit around and wait.

Of course, in the military environment, "fouled" was replaced with another, more graphic F-word, one that was ubiquitous and had become part of our daily military lexicon. Some SNAFUs made us laugh; some pissed us off. Anything could go wrong at any time. Luckily, the safety procedures on the firing line and in places where live ammunition came into play were very effective. On these occasions the programs were pretty tightly controlled. In a few other situations, though, not so much.

———•·•———

Perhaps the most laughable SNAFU occurred during gas-mask training. We were instructed to watch while some Cadre demonstrated the proper masking procedure while walking through a cloud of teargas. Following this, we would all don our bulky vinyl and glass gasmasks to practice the same maneuver. We stood in anticipation while some DIs snapped on their masks and a couple others released the gas. The problem was the guys who released the gas had not checked the wind, so the cloud of gas blew toward them instead of toward their masked companions. It was great fun to watch these guys get a taste of their own medicine as they scrambled in various directions trying to get away from the oncoming gas. In my mind it was a perfect example of the astute if overused cliché, "What goes around comes around."

The most egregious Selective Service or military faux pas involved the treatment of personnel. Some of the GIs now knew they got a raw deal from their draft boards or the military. There was no doubt any number of these troops were upset and bitter, but for the most part they tried to make the best of it. In some cases, however, government testing failed to flag those with serious physical, developmental, or mental health issues. Basic was supposed to weed these guys out, but this seemed to become a low priority when guys were getting chewed up in Vietnam and the army needed all the replacements it could process.

For example, we had a guy with a wonderfully ethnic German surname whom I will call "Pheister." During some initial small talk, he told me he was from Berlin. As a Central New Jersey city kid, I'm thinking Germany. I had little knowledge of the open space and farmland in southern Jersey, and virtually nothing of the history of shipping and mining that once thrived down there, so I was amazed to be told there was a place in South Jersey called Berlin. Laughing, in total surprise, Pheister told me German and Quaker farmers settled there, as well as in Pennsylvania, during the nineteenth century.

Pheister was an amiable fellow, perhaps more than a tad overweight, cheeky, and ruddy faced. Of course, his weight situation alone brought him to the attention of Cadre who were under orders to get us physically fit. He could be treated rather roughly from time to time because he tended to lag behind huffing and puffing.

Pheister said he was a trained x-ray technician. He thought he came into the army with the understanding of doing this important job. He was skeptical about whether this would actually happen, and when he checked he was told there was nothing in his file stating he signed up for medical training. More than likely, he was destined for Advanced Infantry Training with most of the Basic Training company. Apparently, he was just another of those recruits tricked or lied to by a recruiter. Pheister was pretty bitter about this situation and, like me, had spoken with the Company Commander. He was given the same talk I had received and told to bring the issue up at his next duty station. Once again, the Company Commander passed the buck.

Meanwhile, Pheister stayed jovial amid his personal pain, but you could not help feeling sorry for the guy. He also had an unusual and enduring characteristic; he slept with his eyes open! We got a big kick out of him when he slept at night, or especially when he caught forty winks during break time. No one had ever seen anything like this before. He was not sleep-walking; he was dead asleep, but his eyes were wide open. The first-time some poor guy discovered this he yelped. He thought poor Pheister was dead. Soon guys stood around and gawked when poor Pheister was catching some ZZZs.

Pheister also told everyone, including the Company Commander, he was allergic to bee stings. He claimed he told the draft board, but as with others his documentation was inadequate. For some reason he did not get a 4-F medical deferment. Sure enough, one day toward the end of Basic Training, he lost consciousness and collapsed. This was not an unusual occurrence, guys dropped all the time from sunstroke, overexertion, and dehydration. This is exactly what the DIs thought, until Pheister did not respond to an ammonia stick under his nose or to slaps to the face. They had to get him to the hospital. It turns out he had been stung by a bee. Did somebody say, SNAFU?

This was the last time we ever saw him. When we got back to our barracks, his bunk was rolled up and his gear would soon be removed. The scuttlebutt was he ended up as a medical technician. I doubt it; more than likely he was given a medical discharge. In any case, we were happy Pheister was still alive and, even if he was not heading back to the farmlands in southern New Jersey, at least he would finish Basic with another company and be sent to Fort Sam Houston for medical school.

—•—

Years later I learned of Franz Jagerstatter, a simple Austrian farmer under German rule during World War II. Like me, he too confronted a crisis of conscience. Jagerstatter was avidly opposed to Nazism and as a Catholic and Lay Franciscan was committed to a gospel life; one that promoted nonviolence. Like farmers in many countries, his work feeding the nation originally protected him from active military service. But eventually he was summoned for universal military training. Following this, he was granted reserve status and was allowed to continue farming. However, this Basic Training experience reaffirmed and further strengthened his antiwar position. Eventually, the government called him for active duty, but he refused to go and was sent to prison.

Local priests and others tried to convince Jagerstatter to be drafted, perhaps by negotiating a noncombatant role, especially since he not only risked prison but a death sentence. Although he did consider this, Jagerstatter decided his conscience would not allow him to accept a noncombatant role. The only honorable thing for him was to totally resist participation. This had to be an excruciatingly hard decision. He had a wife and three little girls on the farm, but was now imprisoned facing the death penalty.

For this extraordinarily brave decision, he was ostracized and denounced by his community; ultimately, he was beheaded by the Nazis. Jagerstatter is now recognized as a hero and honored by the German people. The Catholic Church recently started him on the path to sainthood.

——•——

Looking back, I wish I knew more about Franz Jagerstatter and Francis of Assisi before I was drafted. But Jagerstatter was never mentioned in religion class, and I simply viewed Francis as a revered saint who loved animals and whose statue was often displayed in gardens and on front lawns worldwide.

Apparently, the first rule for Lay Franciscans was written by Saint Francis himself. The rule did not allow the original Lay brothers to carry lethal weapons. Even though Jagerstatter probably knew of that legacy, over the centuries this requirement eased, now requiring only respect for "the choice of those who because of conscientious objection refuse to bear arms." Knowing this history would have helped my thinking and perhaps changed the way I dealt with the draft and military regulations.

It is important to note during the Vietnam era the American government and military still sentenced some conscientious objectors, resisters, and deserters to prison. However, unlike previous wars, resisters were not sentenced to capital punishment or to extraordinarily long prison sentences.

Back at Fort Dix, training continued week after week: PT, weaponry, formations, formal marching. Most of us lost substantial weight and shaped up physically. The Cadre loosened up a bit on some of the weekends, and I think on one occasion we had a one-day pass. Things generally slowed down on Sunday and guys tended to slip away, some going AWOL off the base. It was fairly easy to leave and enter the fort. At least one Sunday afternoon I jumped a bus and went to a typical GI town next to Fort Dix. It was a little burg called Wrightstown, a sad and sorry little place with a tiny retail area. I suspected it was totally dependent on money spent by GIs and their families.

There were several taverns and shops, one after another, on the dull and tired main drag. For those who needed spiritual comfort, plenty of stores sold bibles and religious goods. There were several jewelry shops for those ready to pop the question to their girlfriends or to send baubles to Mom or their wife.

Then there were the tattoo parlors for the lonely, lost, and inebriated. This was back in the day when tattoos were not something folks got simply to show off body art. Back then, disfiguring yourself with a tattoo was something only drunken sailors did. It was a serious, lifetime commitment; one all too often regretted. Frequently regret came quickly for GIs, as the army frowned on any tattoos not well hidden.

One day, a few of us left the base to join the women in our lives who had driven down to pick us up. There was no trouble getting back on the base. I realized the worst that could happen if I got caught was so-called administrative punishment. That is, having my paltry monthly pay docked or some privileges taken away, or both. Some guys apparently got caught and did get into trouble, but I knew if trainees were careful and showed up for formations and bed check, it would be okay. I was not alone seeing this as a gratifying and exciting experience. At minimum, it offered some small sense of freedom after several weeks under the thumb of the Cadre.

Eventually Basic Training ended as graduation day arrived with some measure of pomp and ceremony. This was a bittersweet event. Most guys were happy Basic was over; many, like me, were apprehensive about what would happen next. Where would we be assigned? What MOS would we get? That day we marched, presented arms, and stood in perfect symmetry, eventually at parade rest when yearbooks and orders were distributed.

Yearbooks? For completing Basic Training, really? Right. About midway through training we were encouraged to buy one and posed for a class picture. Those who were interested in getting away from training for a few hours donned their dress greens, spit shined shoes, polished brass, and posed for the Basic

Training yearbook picture. If you chose not to buy it, just your name, class picture, and military information would appear in the book.

I found myself suffering from something akin to cognitive dissonance. Where the heck *was* I? In the middle of a bad high school nightmare? I was astounded by this tradition; but apparently yearbooks were issued for every graduating Basic Training class. Many guys signed up to participate, especially those going on to Officers Candidate School and those committed to a military career. I understood and certainly respected those decisions. Getting through Basic was no small achievement, but I had no great desire to memorialize it in a yearbook. I joined a small group of guys in my class who decided to opt out of the photo and never purchased one.

———•———

Later that morning the Company Commander had us form up, barked out each name, and announced our next duty station. Virtually all of us heard, "Tigerland, Fort Polk, Louisiana," a training site set up to simulate Southeast Asia. There was a mixture of shock, resignation, and no small measure of pride in the faces of those slated to attend Advanced Infantry Training. I guess it all depended on whether you came to fight or build a career, were resigned to keep your head down and go through the motions or were beginning to resist. I knew I was not there to fight; I knew I was not about to go along to get along by faking my way through it; but I was still unsure about active resistance.

I still was not sure I would be able to stay in the military in any capacity. From time to time, I wondered if my visit to our Company Commander and the strength of my argument would get me assigned to some duty that maybe, just maybe, I could see myself doing—somehow learn to justify the role I would be playing in propagating the war. It was a naïve, foolish feeling of desperation and accommodation.

Then again, I still was not sure if I was serious about standing up for what I believed. Apparently, like Franz Jagerstatter discovered, it is excruciatingly hard to know the right way to be a man, to be a patriot, to oppose a war. All sorts of conflicting thoughts bounced around in my brain. As it turned out, I had much more to learn about death and destruction; but this relentless conundrum would continue to haunt me for quite some time.

PART III

———————•➤•◄•———————

Maggot Days–AIT

With Basic Training over, we were told to pack up our gear and prepare for a flight to Fort Polk for Advanced Infantry Training (AIT). I continued to believe I was in the wrong place and still naively thought I could convince the system of my ongoing opposition to the war. In part, I based this on the immature assumption that my Selective Service record and the appeal made to my previous Commanding Officer would follow me there…and that it meant something.

I called my wife and parents with the news that I was ordered to do advanced military training as an infantryman. Their earlier attempts to get me to compromise if trained as a noncombatant were now irrelevant, as tears and profound expressions of concern surged through the line. Expressions of sadness I could not only hear but see with my mind's eye, sounds and visions ravaging my heart and soul…and I thought Basic Training took a lot out of a guy!

Once again, the choices were to go AWOL and confront eventual arrest, or comply with the order and continue the struggle for discharge at Fort Polk. There was no choice really. I wasn't running, not this time. I locked and loaded, picked up my gear, and got ready to rock 'n' roll. Again.

Seventeenth

Tigerland

In strengthening the sinister side,
I weakened the force of my right side.

Gregory of Narek

We gathered at McGuire Air Force Base in New Jersey to board a propeller-driven airplane for the flight to Fort Polk, Louisiana. Guys sat alone or in small groups on the outskirts of the dusky airstrip as we waited for the aircraft. A thick cloud of youthful anticipation hung in the air. Some guys exhibited a quiet aura of confidence in the adventures coming their way. Others sat hangdog with a visible look of frustration, of being out of control. I suspect I was just in a period of denial and perhaps felt overconfident about being discharged at my next duty station. In any case, I tried not to think about it and just sat there taking it all in. Misery loving company, as all of us, one way or another, dealt with the uncertainties that lie ahead. The relative silence continued on the plane, much like what I experienced months before on the bus taking us from the U.S. Army Reception Center in Newark to Basic Training at Fort Dix.

We were greeted by a blast of heat and thick humidity as we deplaned, one that made you gasp as your entire body immediately oozed water and salt. I looked around while we waited for our duffel bags to be unloaded from cargo. The base was vast, even if the airport was relatively small and nondescript, probably typical for a small airfield. Of course, a large portion of the immediate area had been graded, but vast woodlands flourished out beyond the perimeters. Indeed, I soon learned the base was huge, over 100,000 acres bordered by a national forest.

The trip to the barracks was as uneventful as our arrival. This time there was no one to scream, threaten, or hurry us off the truck. We simply checked in and were given a barracks assignment. The barracks grounds were relatively well cared for and featured thriving St. Augustine grass. The lawn areas were bordered by large boulders brilliantly painted in gleaming white to complement the green grass and reflect the blazing Louisiana sun. Once again, we were assigned to dormitory rooms inside a number of one-or-two-story wooden buildings.

Tigerland itself was designed to replicate a village, or "ville" in Vietnam, specifically designed for jungle warfare training. It featured realistic hooches with thatched roofs, sandbagged bunkers, and narrow trails. It was deliberately built at a military base with semi-tropical vegetation to simulate a jungle-like environment. This, along with the oppressive heat and humidity, was said to mimic the conditions soldiers would experience in Southeast Asia.

Over the weeks we might encounter snakes, tarantulas, armadillos, or wild horses. I never ran into the latter; perhaps our majestic four-legged brothers and sisters knew enough to stay away from the gray, blasted, denuded training sites and the two-legged species causing all sorts of noise and environmental destruction.

———•———

Early on, we were called to formation and welcomed by our new Commanding Officer. He had a strack military bearing, as befitting his rank, but one that did not offer any pretense of pomp and ceremony. The CO proceeded to explain what we should expect to learn and experience over the next few months. He demanded total cooperation and said he would not tolerate his Cadre being disrespected. Indeed, this was the first time I heard someone suggest, "If you don't start no S-H, there won't be no I-T." Most surprisingly of all, he said although treatment and discipline would be stringent, it would be more relaxed than in Basic, especially on Sundays.

The next day I went to see this guy about my situation. Of course, he found nothing in my personnel file from Selective Service and no notes from the previous appeal I made during Basic Training. It was as if all previous attempts to explain my position did not exist, never happened, and in any case were completely irrelevant.

Once again, I stated my position to the CO. I called the war illegal and a violation of the Constitution; that is, the war was undeclared as Congress had abdicated its authority to declare war. I pointed out this was not a defensive war. We were not under attack by the Communists. Indeed, despite the currently popular refrain, the Russians were not coming! By all indications, the way the war was being conducted was immoral and did not meet the Catholic standard of a "Just War." I advised the CO of my receiving the paperwork for conscientious objector status from Selective Service but I had not applied because, although I was opposed to aggressive military action in Vietnam, I was not sure I was able to say I was opposed to "war in any form." Thus, for civic and religious reasons, I thought I should be administratively discharged.

The Commanding Officer listened with respect, and I detected no small measure of amusement. He had nothing new to say other than to reaffirm the tired old lines I heard earlier. Like those before him, he passed the buck when he suggested I do what I had to do here, ship to my next duty station, probably Vietnam, and present my case to my new Company Commander. Surely, he suggested, that officer would understand and perhaps assign me a position with an in-country chaplain.

Parroting the words of my CO in Basic, he stressed we were both here. He had his job to do, which in this case, was to train infantrymen for Vietnam. I had mine, which was to cooperate in training and get used to the idea the chance of being sent anywhere else other than to Vietnam was slim to none. He did not offer any other administrative options and then dismissed me with a threat, saying if I did not abide with his wishes, I would abide in "a world of hurt" and probably spend time in the base stockade.

— • —

I was up in the air about this the entire time I was in AIT. Nevertheless, slowly and steadily, I began to look for another way. I needed to know more. I needed to open my mouth more, maybe not with the officers but with the grunts—the other maggots. I began visiting the base library and making some phone calls. I learned about different civilian and veteran groups taking strong stands against the war. I soon discovered the stuff out there that dealt with resisting the draft, but there was not much on in-service military resistance.

I did learn, however, about several officers who had refused to ship to Vietnam; cases that generated a fair amount of national attention. I researched, wrote letters, and got some responses. I had already engaged with several guys who were trying to come to grips with the war, both in Basic and now in AIT. These conversations would spontaneously erupt in the dorms, at the PX, and during breaks in the field. I listened, and as the weeks went by, I became more outspoken. I gained strength and knowledge from arguments and conversations I had with my peers. No, I was not alone. I learned from them, they learned from me; and I knew somehow, some way, in league with those of my own rank, my own experience, we needed to become the change we hoped to see. But…how? My thoughts went something like this:

So here I am again, in the same place I found myself when first dealing with the Selective Service System. Why had I respected the positions of the men who judged me at the time, and why am I doing so now? But this time there is a certain finality and assurance that my fate has been sealed and, despite my selective opposition to this particular war, I will end up in Southeast Asia.

What to do? It all seemed like such a fait accompli. Do I give up? Cave-in? Is the difference between right and wrong only relative? Regardless, I won't be forced to desert; I won't do it. This is the wrong response to the situation. Perhaps I should go to jail. For what? Defending the Constitution and the separation of powers, for using religious, moral, and ethical teachings I had learned as a legal defense that would ultimately be ignored in a court of law? What was the right path for me? Was this worth going to jail for?

But what is to be done? I need to slow down, to think more deeply about this... meditation, prayer? Meanwhile, I could continue to go through the motions, to learn the maneuvers, the weaponry, the pomp and ceremony; I could make believe I wasn't living a lie, I could shrug off the dehumanizing treatment, the attempts to change us in ways many felt was wrong. I could continue my personal quest to waste as much ammunition as possible. But, in the end, what good would it do when we ultimately would arrive in a country with more bombs and ammunition than anyone could imagine? In the end I am still in the same crazy predicament, I either become an instrument of the war, leave the country, or go to jail.

Eighteenth

— •=• —

The Way the Wind Blows

If I should walk in the valley of darkness,
no evil will I fear.

Psalm 23

The daily routine of reveille, running, PT, training, and duty assignment filled our days. Early on, the name calling and belittling continued, but it was more like hard-core high school gym teachers asserting their authority. Now and again, we were treated like the maggots we were said to be. Nevertheless, things steadily eased up; the training became much more focused on the art of infantry maneuvers and weaponry than it was on demeaning mind-games.

That said, Advanced Infantry Training (AIT) was no party, and we were usually on a tight leash, but it was refreshingly different given what we had already gone through. For example, we were rarely woken up in the middle of the night for meaningless formations, and never just for the sport of it. There were fewer spot inspections and a bit less personal degradation. The screaming and the urgent call to hurry-up-and-wait still ruled, and once again we double-timed it everywhere.

Let me be clear, the training was rugged and the everyday treatment was usually harsh, sometimes brutal. There still seemed to be many deeply damaged guys around, not just among the trainees but in no small measure in the Cadre. Let's put it this way, if you were back home on the block, whether in a city or in a small country town, you could choose to avoid these guys or not. But many of us felt trapped, often under the control of those struggling with personal demons or traveling on a darker side. Superiors could be arbitrary in their treatment of others, and all too often vicious in the application of the training program. Despite all the talk of military honor and dignity, we were in constant contact with less than honorable rogues and behaviors that simply would not be tolerated in civil society.

———••———

On the positive side, we felt we were no longer just maggots. We were in the club; we were now called *grunts,* that is, infantry soldiers. The Drill Instructors (DIs) defined a grunt as someone in combat arms who marches long distances, carries heavy packs, and well, grunts. Still, the indignities we suffered were real and personal; for many, they produced anger and were painful; but lest we forget, perpetual anger was what we were supposed to feel, partly by seeing the faces of the enemy in the faces of the DIs.

Some moments could be bittersweet, like when we jogged. We always ran in heavy black boots that weighed guys down. Most trainees, myself included, had never jogged before. On the other hand, some guys had been on high school track teams and fared better. Most of us got used to it pretty quickly, helping buddies along who were having more difficulty.

I came to like it; being out in the fresh air, challenging myself, feeling my lungs and legs come into sync, now and again escaping inside myself and going silent in thought. Younger Cadre jogged with the troops, calling cadence to motivate us while displaying their spirited rhyming skills. Their sing-song call and our response corresponded with the "your left, your right, your left, right, left" pounding of our prancing feet.

We never really knew what these Cadre guys were going to come out with; it was akin to modern rap music and could be hilarious, yet often violent and misogynistic; sometimes it was simple encouragement. For example, they would draw us into harmony with a call like:

Here we go!

And we would respond,
Here we go!

The Cadre call and troop response continued:

Gotta' go!
Gotta' go!

All the way!
All the way!

Sound Off!
One, two!

Sound Off!
Three, four!

Bring it on down!
One, two, three, four.
One. Two. Three Four!

Other times it was pure military motivation, urging troops
to aspire to greater glory in the Green Berets or in other presti-
gious units, for example:

I want to be an airborne Ranger!
I want to be an airborne Ranger!

I want to live a life of danger!
I want to live a life of danger!

Or, to reinforce just why we were there in Tigerland:

Gotta' kill!
Gotta' kill

Vietcong!
Vietcong!

Have to kill!
Have to kill

Vietcong!
Vietcong!

Wanna' kill!
Wanna' kill

Vietcong!
Vietcong!

Frequently, cadence delved into sexuality, glorifying sexual conquest or lambasting girlfriends or wives who were said to be fooling around with that hated, draft-dodging Lothario back home, Jody on the Block. All this would definitely get the blood and laughter flowing as we jogged along. For example, one bawdy introductory stanza went:

I got a girl and her name is Sue!
I got a girl and her name is Sue!

She won't do it, but her sister do!
She won't do it, but her sister do!

The names and racy activities changed as the cadence got more risqué, but you get the picture and can fill in the blanks.

Here in Tigerland, every man was said to be a tiger, and this message was reinforced in word and signage. Motivational signs appeared here and there, often promoting aggressiveness and the use of firepower. (My favorite being the ridiculously poetic call to "Bong the Cong.") Others featured scowling images of Viet Cong soldiers replete in straw hats and black pajamas with captions identifying them as the enemy.

Life settled into a regular routine and we found ourselves with a bit of free time—especially for a few hours some evenings, late Saturday afternoon, and most of Sunday. I continued to struggle, finding myself in an alternative universe, one diametrically opposed to my thinking and beliefs. I was deeply angry, lost, and confused, and looked for some outlets. I found some at the base PX, where nobody cared how old you were and cans of beers sold for ten or fifteen cents. I found myself joining some other guys who periodically fortified themselves against the challenges and uncertainty to come.

I also found some serenity by dropping into a chapel, or by experimenting with meditation, sometimes slipping into the woods for a few minutes at break times. I was too young to consider this a consciously spiritual practice, but I thought about it rather as more of a countercultural thing. It was a way to relax, if not escape, a technique then gaining some traction in the youth culture and in society in general. I had no idea what I was doing. I would just sit quietly, eyes closed, trying to pay attention to my breathing, trying to shut out everything around me. It brought some comfort, and sometimes I was able to still my worried mind.

Beyond escaping into myself, I continued to actively engage my peers by speaking out against the war. I tended to gather with guys of divergent views who liked to sit around and talk about the legitimacy of the war and our role in it. These were not necessarily intellectuals, but smart guys who had given their situation and the current geopolitical realities deep thought.

I became friends with a young man named Dennis who had enlisted, and after AIT was headed to Officers Candidate School. We bunked in the same barracks during Basic Training and were in the same platoon in AIT. We talked about and debated the war, often just the two of us and sometimes in small groups. Dennis certainly had his doubts about the war but had strong arguments about the need for both civilians and troops to be supportive during wartime, to trust our leadership, and serve the country by being part of the war. Dennis was well-read and eloquent when it came to debating civic and religious questions, patriotism, nonviolence, Saint Augustine's Just War Theory, and general Christian theology. It was great. We would go around and around, picking the issues apart, considering each other's strongly held positions, but with deep respect and ongoing interest in opposing views. Yet we never came to consensus.

Then there was Bill. We also became buddies. He was a kind and gentle fellow, but tough enough when he had to be. Like me, he married young. Back at Fort Dix, we met our wives and hung out together a couple of times. In many ways, Bill represented the great mass of troops who were caught up in the war. He was neither a gung-ho supporter of the war nor an active or quiet war resister. Like so many of us, he was just an average guy caught up in a macho, flag-waving, militaristic tradition that found us in a situation we did not understand and could not control. I will never forget a statement he made at the end of one of our many conversations; one that totally summed up the frustration and resignation of a growing number of troops. That day he simply and honestly declared, "I don't want to hurt anybody, and I don't want to die; but what am I going to do?" Bill was killed in Vietnam about a year later, memorialized on line 19W, 54, on the Vietnam Veterans Memorial in Washington, DC.

Our small group conversations could also be heated, political, and sometimes deeply philosophical. We rehashed the legality and morality the war, the pros and cons of participating, often going past the geopolitics and delving into issues related to Christian responsibility. Was there any value in the statement, "My country right or wrong," especially if we did not have a true foreign enemy but perhaps did have a domestic one putting our generation in this position? Where was the real fight, what was the appropriate, patriotic thing to do? What was the Bible trying to tell us about the right and wrong of all this? And, in the days before it became a catchword, quite simply, "What would Jesus do?"

I found all this compelling and I learned a lot. We had vast disagreements; some wanted to go to Vietnam, others wanted a military career and infantry training would punch their tickets to a higher rank and greater opportunities. Others knew they would head to Southeast Asia after they finished Officers Candidate School. On the other hand, several of us were angry and disillusioned and wanted no part of the war or—to my initial surprise—with the growing "war against the war." Many, feeling powerless, were just resigned to fate.

Our "rap groups," as we called them, were thoughtful, refreshing, and in the eyes of the brass alarmingly conspiratorial. I certainly learned from these interactions and could not get enough of them. Whether draftee or regular army, the guys in these groups respected one another. We never came to blows, and no one informed the Cadre of the so-called "bad apples" in the group.

Enlightened and encouraged, I began to feel less out of control; I was not so alone, not so lost. My internal dialogues went something like this:

You know what? I can find ways to round out, educate, and strengthen myself; and I need to keep doing this, to do something different to find ways to get the brass to listen to me—more, to listen to all of us. Right, it's okay, I can get through the program and learn the weaponry. Why not? It's not going to change me, is it? And what of the upcoming training, it can't be all bad—reading a compass, escape and survival—could be handy. Nevertheless, beyond all this I need to pursue a different personal discipline, an interior form of training—getting focused, learning more, and not going it alone—I need to get locked and loaded for some other sort of combat.

———— • ————

Tools of the Trade

> He was now one of the crowd he had joined,
> and a genuine companion of those who had led him there.
>
> Augustine of Hippo

The things we mastered on the books:

- M-14 Rifle;
- M-16 Rifle;
- KA-Bar Fighting Knife;
- M-6 bayonet for the M-14;
- M-7 Bayonet for the M-16;
- .45 Caliber Pistol;
- M-30 Machine Gun;
- M-50 Machine Gun;
- Fragmentation and Smoke Grenades;
- M-72 Light Anti-Tank Weapon;
- M-79 Grenade Launcher;

- M-18A1 Claymore Mine;
- C-4 Plastic Explosive;
- CS Riot Gas with Gas Masks;
- Hand-to-Hand Combat, including snapping necks from behind;
- Armored Personnel Carrier and Helicopter details and maneuvers.

The things we mastered off the books:

- The Garrote;
- Electric Shock Treatments.

———•———

During Advanced Infantry Training (AIT), troops were introduced to the varied small-arms weaponry used by infantry soldiers. Early on, we were issued and practiced shooting the M-16 assault rifle. Unlike the M-14 we used in Basic, the M-16 was lightweight with a plastic composite stock and a shorter barrel also encased in plastic. Some guys liked to call the M-16 a "toy gun," as it resembled the plastic weapons we played with as kids. It used 5.66 mm full metal jacket rounds, which we were told were comparable to the ammunition used by various allies.

Because the M-16 had no reddish-brown heavy wood on the stock and barrel it only weighed about seven pounds fully loaded. When we first got it, we used it solely on the firing line, learning how to fire in various positions similar to what we learned in Basic Training. At first, we fired in semi-automatic mode to maximize accuracy during target practice. In a short time however, we were permitted to fire the weapon on automatic. The trigger was delicate, so a clip of twenty rounds would empty quickly when you held the trigger down.

We were strongly advised not to adopt the very cool looking stance often used in the movies, where weapons are fired from the hip rather than from proper firing positions. The Cadre dismissively called this the "John Wayne Position." It looked good on screen but was totally useless for zeroing in on targets. We were strongly urged to never even think about firing the weapon this way.

The raw power of the M-16 is indescribable; you snapped the trigger and the ammunition cartridge emptied as you unleashed all kinds of fury at your intended target. One instructor blasted a full cartridge into a cinderblock, turning it into small rocks and gravel. I could only imagine the damage it could do to a human body. At the firing range, we were able to use any number of rounds; so, naïvely sticking to my plan, I figured if I'm going to waste ammunition, this was a good way to get it done. The M-16 rifle became ubiquitous; we never again used the M-14. Imposing, futuristic, and nasty, it was one lean, mean, killing machine.

There was a bayonet available for the M-16, but we were told the plastic stock made it much too frail for sustained hand-to-hand combat. We were again reassured that unless a position had been overrun or we were ordered to take a hill, the chances of using the bayonet were slim to none. One Drill Instructor (DI), a veteran of the war, claimed, "We don't attack hills anymore, we call in the Air Force and they blow it away." Sadly, his experience was not entirely prescient. The bloody battle for Hill #937, Hamburger Hill, happened just a few months later in May 1969.

As we moved on, we were given training in the use of the M-79 grenade launcher, nicknamed "The Thumper," a mortar-like rifle that fired grenades. It was used very much like a mortar but was a portable weapon issued to small platoons and was not mounted on the ground. Carried like a rifle, it had a sling allowing one to angle it on the ground to fire at a position or at personnel. Guys could also shoot from the shoulder, but we practiced targeting with the sling. We got our hands on this weapon only a couple times and, as I recall, I blasted away as many projectiles as I could toward the targets set up on the lifeless, black earth in the distance.

Troops also learned how to find and disable the standard landmines used by the North Vietnamese Army and the VC. To find them, you snake-walked across the ground as if crawling under barbed wire or through heavy rifle or machine gun fire. Using a KA-bar or a bayonet, guys would gently poke the ground in the area immediately in front of them hoping it was unmined and safe enough to use as a trail. If a landmine was found, an explosives expert would usually be called to dismantle it.

The M-18 Claymore Anti-Personnel Mine was a rectangular shaped defensive weapon that was not buried but rather stood above ground on a short tripod. A directional mine, an array of them would be angled out several yards in front of a defensive perimeter. The Claymore had a failsafe triggering mechanism requiring three pushes to set it off. When fired, hundreds of small metal pellets blasted out, shredding everything and anything in its path. Pellets could travel as much as fifty yards. It was loud and extremely deadly. Think of the Civil War-era canister shot packed with iron balls, nails, or scrap metal used to cripple and kill oncoming troops. The Claymore training involved setting them up correctly, making sure they were pointed in the right direction (a serious and on-going problem), and learning how to trigger and fire the device.

—•—

We were given the chance to fire one M-72 Light Anti-Tank Weapon (LAW). Only one round, they said, because it was a very expensive piece of equipment. The M-72 was a mini-bazooka, much like a recoilless rifle. Similar to earlier two-man models, this one-man version was used to stop tanks, trucks, and personnel carriers, or to blast emplacements. At about six pounds and a yard long, the M-72 was extremely light and mobile. It was billed as a single-shot disposable weapon; in combat situations troops would fire the weapon and were supposed to destroy the launching tube before moving on. We were given one shot each so we could learn what it sounded like, felt like, and did. In this case, I was unable to waste any additional ordinance, but I was gratified to know the M-72 units we fired probably would not be used again. We practiced shooting at pock-holed vehicles out in the distance. I remember it being extremely loud and effective when a GI actually hit a target. Bottom line: You would definitely be in a world of hurt if you were on the receiving end of a projectile launched by this deadly machine.

Over time, we experienced all these weapons and more, learning to assemble and dismantle most. We fired pistols and machine guns, handled C-4 Plastic Explosives, and practiced boarding and jumping off grounded helicopters we called "Choppers." The training was comprehensive, demanding, and sometimes rather complicated. But for the most part, the actual weapons training was relatively uneventful. Thankfully, nobody got hurt and the DIs performed more like instructors than harsh taskmasters.

—•—

Then one day we were given grenade training. That day, I stepped into a grenade throwing pit to practice tossing two or three hand grenades. The entire area was about ten feet square by about six feet high. The walls of the interior were sandbagged and had a three-foot wide ditch dug along the entire front of the throwing area. The ditch was several feet deep, dug there in case a grenade was dropped. This enabled the instructor or the trainee to kick a live grenade into the hole, forcing the blast to go straight up rather than out toward us as we hit the ground. A periscope was available in the front of the bunker to view the blast area and a distant pole served as a target.

The short yet muscular guy who gave this training was a returned Vietnam combat veteran; he was not a happy guy. Besides being bored and disconnected, his body language exhibited both anger and arrogance. He spoke crisply and dismissively and demanded absolute cooperation as we were handling very dangerous ordnance. His gruff, angry words demonstrated he did not like trainees. I'd seen this before. His overall demeanor made red flags of caution start snapping in my brain and put me on high alert. This was a no-nonsense guy, so I knew I had to pay close attention and keep my mouth shut. To me, he was like a chunk of fragile C-4 Plastic Explosive; that is, with the slightest vibration his body and soul would explode into a murderous rage. From where I stood and what I soon experienced, I imagined he was trending toward a "P" on my personal Socio-path-Psychopath scale, emoting a turbulent form of Post-Traumatic Stress Disorder neither one of us even knew existed.

First, he demonstrated the correct way to hold the grenade and how to prepare it before letting it fly. He modeled several sequential steps. Step one was to hold the grenade and lever, then pull out the circular safety pin and release the lever. At that point you had three seconds to throw before it would explode. He mimicked the process and how to lob it from a standing position.

I was to reproduce all of these moves each time I threw one of the grenades. First, I was ordered to gaze into the periscope to look at the blast area. As I peered out, I flashed back to those black and white photographs taken of trench warfare in World War I. For as far as I could see, nothing out there lived. The gray soil much like the bottom of a polluted lake; the lifeless earth had turned gray from a daily dose of exploded ordnance. The target, a simple white pole, was some yards away, an other-worldly surrogate for the trees and foliage no longer living there.

I took my first grenade and thought I duplicated each of the DI's movements. I assumed the throwing position, pulled the pin while holding the lever, tossed the pin aside, cocked my arm, let go of the lever, and lobbed the grenade toward the pole. As I reached into my satchel for another grenade I was broadsided and knocked to the ground. The instructor picked me up by my fatigues and slammed me against the wall of the bunker; dazed, I crumpled to the floor. Screaming at the top of his lungs he demanded I get the hell out of there or he was going to kill me.

Shocked and speechless, I picked myself up, threw the grenade satchel down and stormed out of the bunker. Thankfully, I had enough good sense not to challenge him. I was baffled, shocked, and murderously angry with him and at myself. I was red-hot, perhaps more out of control than any time in my young life. On top of that I was bewildered, unsure of what I had done wrong.

On the way back to our barracks I kept replaying the experience over and over in my head, trying to understand what mistake I supposedly made. I was still livid when I got there, stuck in some truly dangerous place between my ears. I was obsessed and totally forgot about my commitment to not let anything that happened change me in any way.

Then I lost it. While stripping down my gear I grabbed my entrenchment tool and threw it into the door at the end of the dorm, cursing, screaming, and complaining about the insanity of it all. No one was hurt, but it sure got their attention. I was soon escorted out of there to confront a whole bunch of questions from a military shrink. After making me sit around to cool off, he concluded I was just letting off some steam and said I was suffering from some sort of "adult adjustment disorder." He simply sent me back to my unit.

When I finally got back to the barracks, the damaged door had been replaced, and for a couple days the DIs pretty much avoided getting overly confrontational with me. I tried not to obsess over this event, but I was still shocked by my reaction and kept replaying it in my head. Mostly, I was very frustrated for having released my inner maniac and for letting that violent GI get to me.

I learned a few things that day. First, I did not want to be like that guy; I did not ever want to be the guy who lost control of his anger the way he had. But in no small measure I *had* become like him. Once again, I let them get to me. I had dropped the ball and the result was violent and dramatic. In a military context, this outburst was misdirected, done in the wrong place; that rage was really supposed to be released in Vietnam. I shuddered to think I was becoming just another guy steadily edging up to at least "S" on my imaginary mental health scale.

That day, I encountered a very damaged and dangerous guy. Over the years I wondered if he was able to survive outside a militaristic environment. Like so many suffering guys did he always walk on a razor's edge, addicted to perilous adventures until something or someone took him off the board? Over the years, I wondered if he had become one of the walking wounded, carrying a heavy load and grunting through life…just another casualty of the Vietnam War.

Twentieth

— •◆• —

Men Against Fire

In your eyes I have become a problem to myself,
and that is my sickness

Augustine of Hippo

In addition to weapons training, Army Infantry Training (AIT) involved practicing the techniques of patrolling, maneuvering, operating ambushes, securing positions, and escape and evasion. We also had a brief session on the Law of Land Warfare, that is, international law concerning behavior, and the rules of military engagement during a war. These formal topics were supplemented with exposure to more informal material. This stuff was off the books, especially personal survival techniques given to us by young Drill Instructors (DIs) who had returned from Vietnam. Many of these Sergeants were just a few years older than most of the trainees. Several of them had only a year or two left on their enlistments after being trained as instructors; others planned on having a military career. Sometimes, after formal training, a number of these guys shared their personal views. For some, engaging in combat became secondary as they focused more on personal survival, taking care of their buddies, and getting everyone home in one piece.

Now "back in the world", these young DIs wanted to teach trainees official and unofficial skills to help them survive a tour in Southeast Asia; skills ranging from exposure to weaponry and maneuvers to taking all necessary means—official and unofficial—to survive the experience.

Some told of tactics used to avoid confrontation with the enemy. For example, they told stories about finding ways to manipulate young, ambitious First Lieutenants. These included looking for ways to slow down paperwork or assignments, or finding ways around orders they considered to be ridiculous or dangerous.

———•———

Formal instruction in AIT, as in Basic, followed training requirements listed in various field manuals. Instructors were charged with presenting the material and many took this seriously, knowing we would end up in very difficult situations. Still, other techniques hinted at a darker side, like the use of illegal methods to extract information from prisoners. Indeed, on the same day we had Law of Land Warfare Training, one DI demonstrated how to extract information from captives by administering electrical shocks using simple wires and a battery.

Another DI once demonstrated the use of a garrote; said to be useful when one had to dispatch someone quietly, so a unit's position was not revealed. As I understood it, the garrote was not standard military issued equipment. Rather, it consisted of a jerry-rigged rope or metal cord with handles on each end. Holding a handle in each hand, you snapped the wiring over the head and around the neck, pulled and twisted the wire to either choke adversaries or take them down, perhaps plunging a KA-bar knife into the body. Much more effective they said, than our hand-to-hand training, which taught us how to snap one's neck from behind. Quiet. Up close. Deadly...like some of us were becoming.

—•—

Once, a young officer told us we trainees were the beneficiaries of a study conducted by a military sociologist immediately after World War II. According to him, what we were learning and how we were being taught was partially due to the work of General S.L.A. Marshall, who looked into the battlefield behavior of infantrymen during combat.

As part of his research, Marshall interviewed a large sample of infantrymen, officers, and Cadre. The results of his study, *Men Against Fire: The Problem of Battle Command in Future Wars* was published in 1947. According to Marshall, only twenty-five percent of troops in a combat situation fired their weapons, and when they engaged did not generate heavy fire. Some hunkered down, some freaked out, some waited for instruction, some fired periodically, but not for effect. Marshall promoted new training methods to get infantrymen to take greater initiative and participate more fully in battle.

The new efficiencies in warfare he promoted included increased discipline among troops, especially in the production of overwhelming firepower. In Marshall's view, soldiers needed to be conditioned better to see themselves as invincible and recognize the killing power of weaponry and sustained fire. For him, training needed to make infantrymen more aggressive while incorporating a sense of unity, companionship, and dependence on one another.

We were told in Korea, experiments using these training methods brought the active use of weapons in combat to about 55%. Additional training refinements led us to where we were today, further emphasizing the need for more aggression and firepower in battle situations.

I sat there amazed. I could not believe what I was hearing. I'm thinking, *you mean, in my own personal quest to waste as much ammunition as possible I was actually doing what was unspoken yet expected? We were supposed to increase the rate of fire, not necessarily just fire for effect. No wonder nobody tried to stop me or suggest, as they often did in other matters, I was wasting precious taxpayer resources. We were all supposed to do this. To "Bong the Cong!" To "light the place up!" To shred flora, fauna, facilities, foe, or friend unfortunate enough to be in the free-fire zone.*

Talk about naivety. Talk about a wake-up call.

Twenty-First

---●----

Paradox Days

And though I wear a uniform,
I was not born to fight.
All these wounded boys you lie beside
Goodnight, my friends, goodnight.

Leonard Cohen

As the weeks in Advanced Infantry Training (AIT) dragged on, I noticed some guys seemed to be getting bolder and acting out in various ways. They were not publicly disobeying orders, nor could you call this "organized resistance." These actions certainly were not sabotage when compared to purposely disabling vehicles or actual riots like one that occurred in August 1968 at the Long Bing Jail in Vietnam. At Long Bing, the overcrowded and understaffed military stockade exploded into violence and a fiery rage. Prisoners attacked guards and exacted retribution from other inmates in an incident having both racial and anti-military overtones.

Now, just a couple of month later, many of us were aware of some other publicized incidents of resistance that occurred in the last few years. Also, some of us knew about returning Vietnam vets who organized themselves as the Vietnam Veterans Against the War, and there were rumors of underground GI newspapers being printed and distributed furtively on some bases.

I did not see anything like this at Fort Polk. I did note the occasional attempts to make life more complicated for officers and Cadre, like fabricating incompetence, purposeful delays, covert graffiti, and mild incidents of disobedience.

———•———

For example, there was a flowchart on the wall at the main landing of our barracks that included a picture of the President of the United States, the Chief of Staff of the U.S. Army, and the Commanding Officer of the base—with lines connecting him to all the Commanding Officers of the training company. The title of the chart, *Chain of Command*, appeared above the pictures, stenciled in a bold 36-font military script. The chart gave troops a sense of who was supposed to be responsible for what and how authority flowed from the Commander-in-Chief (i.e., POTUS) all the way down to our unit.

One day, as we poured down the stairs, the crowd slowed and the line backed up. I heard laughter break out below me and as we reached the landing, I joined the others looking at the chart. Someone had crossed out the word *Command* and replaced it with the word *Bondage,* implying a Chain of Bondage stretching from our training company all the way up to the highest office in the nation.

In a short time, of course, it was gone; but we all saw it, and it was clear from the laughter and chatter the many of the guys agreed with the new and improved signage. For a lot of us, this was terrific!

—•—

Each night, a group of guys was assigned fire watch, one hour each from lights-out until reveille. The job involved patrolling the grounds in the immediate area and walking through each building, making sure all was well. In those days, guys were allowed to smoke in the barracks and put their butts out in red-painted, dirt-filled coffee tins called "butt cans." These were ancient wooden barracks and, despite numerous warnings, some men smoked in bed. So, most of us took fire watch pretty seriously.

I slept in full fatigues the nights I was assigned fire watch. Actually, I did this quite often. Tonight, I wanted to be ready when the last watch came to wake me; so I slept in fatigues, then I just had to pull on my boots. Except for some snoring, it was dead quiet in our barracks, an improbable and deceptive sense of peace in a normally noisy, angry, and chaotic environment.

—•—

That night, I yanked on my boots and swept through our area first, my light shining left to right, just ahead of my quiet, deliberate steps. I knew the guys in the bunks were as exhausted as I was, so I tried hard not to bump into things or inadvertently wake somebody up. All seemed well; there were no problems here.

I stepped out of our barracks and into the pitch-black, sticky-hot Louisiana night. Sleepy and exhausted, I stopped to clear my head. I leaned against a wooden post that held up the porch roof and savored the welcome quietness now blanketing the training grounds. The night sky was clear, the brilliance of the moon and stars competing only with the small porch lights that illuminated the fronts of each building. Out in the inky darkness a distant call of an owl punctuated the silence as crickets chirped their nightly song. It was peaceful and refreshing. I was tired and my body ached from the day's exercise and activities, but I was glad to be out there alone and accepted fire watch as a necessary and important duty.

That night reminded me of the time I was in elementary school, maybe ten to twelve years old, serving as a patrol boy before and after school. The job was to stop children at the crosswalks and help them cross the street safely, keeping the friskier ones from running out into busy traffic. The Safety Patrol was identified by a badge and a white sash belted around our waists. Uniformed members of the local police department came to our school once a year, handed out new belts, and taught the proper procedure for helping kids cross safely. I remember how cute and alluring the little girls appeared to me and how I watched out for and was strangely drawn to them, especially one named Janet, who for some mysterious reason nicknamed me "Raspberries."

Later, as a young man still learning about adult love, I wondered how that attraction came to be, how that magnetism could run so deep. *Was it all just a biological imperative that began raising its head early in life? Then again, was love more than that, something divine, something imparted to all at life's first quickening? Was love part of what we human beings are… something beyond science* and human religion… the ubiquitous, intangible stuff of which we are made?

Another forlorn hoot of the owl brought me out of myself and into this place of tears, fear, hatred, and anger; back to the heart and soul shattering reality of being in a place all too often devoid of human kindness. I shuddered to think this anger and aggression might also be inherent, part of our animal nature, a percentage of our human DNA.

———•———

Well then, I thought, *It's the middle of the night, time to patrol the barracks.* I stepped off the porch into the thick, wet air and headed off for the next building. All was clear as I continued my rounds in and about each of the five or six barracks assigned to our trainee unit. No smoke, no fire, no activity other than the snoring and rustling of weary troops. But then, something just outside the flashlight beam caught my eye. It was a pile of some sort, heaped up on one of the bunks. I moved closer shining additional light over the area. I quickly realized I stumbled on two guys intertwined, sleeping together. These guys seemed to be fully clothed, stone asleep, face to face, arm over arm.

Feeling like some sort of voyeur, my first reaction was to quickly move the light off the bunk as I stepped back so not to roust them. My second reaction was something like, *Oh my God, what if one of the other fire watchers sees these guys? What if they turn them in?* If somebody reported these men, I knew what the probable consequences were.

There was a great deal of homophobia in society and in the military during those years. Indeed, those who manifested homosexual behavior or so called "gender-identity disorders" were exempt from the draft, could not enlist, and were discharged from the military if discovered.

But in this moment, I saw it differently. I realized I stumbled on the only peaceful, meaningful, loving interaction I had seen on base. Sure, I did not really know if these guys were gay; perhaps they were just partying earlier and had fallen together into some exhausted, stony stupor. Nevertheless, it looked peaceful, comfortable, and yes loving.

I finished my inspection, returned to the barracks, and woke up the next guy on fire watch. As I hit the sack, I prayed the two guys I found would go undiscovered and would be safe from attack by homophobic trainees or Cadre. Or, if discovered and were gay, I hoped they would be administratively discharged and spared from the war. For whatever peace or comfort they gave to themselves that night, they had also given to me—their unwilling but grateful voyeur. Here, in this place of meanness and random cruelty, they reminded me the spark of loving kindness can always kindle and burn bright, no matter how horrible the situation, no matter how dark the darkness. You just had to keep watch and, when found, shine your light on it.

Twenty-Second

Epiphanies

Those who know themselves are enlightened.

Lao Tzu

As part of the Advanced Infantry Training program, the Cadre were required to deliver a few days of hand-to-hand combat training. One day, we used pugil sticks as faux rifles. The pugil stick session taught troops rudimentary parry and thrust moves. Then for a couple of days, we were taught karate or jujitsu tactics. These techniques were to be used if a soldier was under assault and unable to shoot attackers or run them through with a bayonet. Both trainings were meant to teach what it meant to be in a one-to-one fight and to generate aggression and excitement about doing so.

The Drill Instructors demonstrated how to deflect blows from a rifle stock or bayonet and to use any means necessary to disable an adversary, including hitting below the belt. Think dirty kickboxing with sticks. Pugil sticks were long wooden poles, much like a broomstick but with padded ends covered with vinyl to protect personnel. Guys battled in a makeshift boxing ring set up on the field; the rest of the troops gathered around to cheer each match. Guys squared off and went to poking at and ultimately smashing one another. If one troop went down, the other combatant won. If both made it through the allotted time, it was a draw; the battered combatants then headed back to join the crowd.

If lucky, you would be evenly matched, take the blows, scrap until a draw, and walk away. Now and then, though, guys were matched up with one of the trainees who was hard-core, usually an antagonistic street fighter. Or worse, being matched with a gung-ho, DI-wanna-be bully who often picked on or belittled his peers. Sort of like a nasty high-school senior who took pleasure in terrorizing freshmen.

———•—

That day I got assigned to spar with one of those nasty guys. I was put up against one of the most arrogant, disagreeable, and genuinely nasty men in the company. He had a chip on his shoulder the size of a boulder and often preyed on other trainees for sport or to puff up his already oversized ego. He struck me as one of those wayward kids who was always in trouble. The ones who were given a choice between going into the military or to jail—and chose the former. I imagined some judge decided this kid "needed discipline." Right. What better way to straighten him out than by exposing him to more browbeating, violence, and weaponry? Go figure. In any case, until that day I stayed clear of him, much like I did with several other tempestuous members of the Cadre.

When we squared off in the ring, I heard a few yelps of encouragement over the howls of the generally amused masses. I suspect enough of them had previously felt this guy's wrath and were hoping to see him get smacked around a bit. We assumed the starting position; the DI yelled, "Go!" Tentatively, we danced around and traded glancing blows. Then, thinking of all the underdogs this guy bullied, I proceeded to exact some vengeance. He went down hard. When I returned to the crowd, some of the guys who were victims of this Tasmanian devil patted me on the back for exacting justice.

But soon, I came to my senses and realized what I had done. Yet again, I had allowed myself to be disassociated with who I was raised to be. It was as if I now traveled with an alter-ego, the real me, and some sort of inner antediluvian hunter-gatherer who was always on guard and ready to take over my body. How easy it was to slip into vengeance. I could have adopted more of a defensive posture with this guy, parrying thrusts while striking light blows until we timed out. But I didn't. That other part of me wanted a piece of the guy, and I exacted revenge. I let my inner beast out. I got with the program. More accurately, the program got to me.

━ ● ━

I missed the first day of karate training due to Kitchen Police duty. There were no make-up sessions. On the second day, the Cadre gave a quick review of the previous day's lesson and demonstrated some new positions and moves. I watched in complete disbelief and had to laugh because it seemed just so ridiculously inadequate. Everything was pro forma, by the book, nothing more than a session that could be checked off as "accomplished," training perfectly suited for staging a Hollywood fight scene. It seemed to be absolutely meaningless and totally worthless. Who becomes familiar with martial arts in just two days?

Again, we were mostly city kids assuming positions and making moves that looked absolutely sophomoric and ridiculous; in no way would this experience help troops defend themselves in combat or when they were back out in the streets. Yet, as always, the Cadre had to present the material and the trainees had to get with the program.

Still, the DIs took karate training seriously, and it was clear a couple of them knew what they were doing. That day the session instructor was our unit's boisterous, occasionally drunk, very overweight DI, a guy who was rumored to be a three-tour veteran of Vietnam. More than most, this guy demanded our respect and kept us under his thumb. His words were vicious, his punishments severe. He was also said to be a "short-timer," soon to retire. Sober or smelling of alcohol, he could be brutal in the castigation and punishment he handed out.

Because I missed the first day's lesson, I was laying low, going through the motions and trying to be nondescript. Suddenly, in total disbelief, I was assigned to demonstrate my karate skills by sparring with this humongous DI. It was David versus Goliath, but I had no pebbles for my slingshot. Queuing up, I did my best to pose for the challenge; but quicker than you can say "In-A-Gadda-Da-Vida," I found myself flat on my back as screams poured from the DI and nervous laughter came from some grunts who had not yet been dispatched and humiliated.

You know what? It *was* funny. Indeed, the entire exercise was a joke; but at that moment, I stomped away angrily. The day before, I was on KP doing something meaningful; today I was being turned into a pretzel. Sulking, I wanted revenge for this and other indignities; but there was nothing for it. Again, a key part of "the program" was to turn the anger and resentment we had for the Cadre toward the enemy. It was working, even if I was in denial.

—•—

Soon after, we were trucked out to a field to practice guarding perimeters. After the presentation, half of us were issued rifles and assigned to sandbagged foxholes. Curiously, there were no paper targets scattered about and this time we were not issued any rounds. The rest of the trainees were issued empty weapons and assigned to be a faux enemy. They were to move about in distant trees, camouflage themselves, and then sneak toward the tree line as if they were preparing to attack. Our mission inside the foxholes was to stay alert, scan the area, point our weapons in the direction of any moving target, and as I recall, verbally acknowledge when we saw and "killed" an enemy trying to move into position.

It was quiet for a long, long time as our attackers moved into position. Suddenly, our DI, the notorious jungle fighter, blew his cover, his elephantine frame more apparent amid forest and flora. He was crouching near the edge of the tree line, but not nearly enough to camouflage his mass. I was still seething over our sparring match and my eyes lit up when I saw him. I could not believe it. There he was, the "face of the enemy." The army mantra "Don't think, do" clicked in. Instinctively, I picked up my empty weapon and looked down the barrel. He was perfectly in range, framed in my sights. Now considered a "Sharpshooter," I knew he was mine. These days folks would call this a "kill shot."

Losing myself, I became acutely aware I really could squeeze the trigger. I could exact justice. I felt it. I knew it. We were taught once you pull the trigger on an M-16, especially on automatic, a human being in your sights is reduced to a pink haze; blood fills the air and floats in the breeze as stray shots tear off body parts, reducing what was once a person into bloody lumps of oozing flesh—fresh meat for those tiny, hungry maggots whose moniker we carried.

But wait, I had no ammunition! Now thinking clearly, my conscience kicked in. Thank God. What was I doing? I put down the weapon and stared into the distance until the exercise was over. It dawned on me there might be a reason why there were no targets and we were not issued ammo. Perhaps the Cadre was afraid some vengeful maggot just might whack somebody, a DI or a peer they hated.

I did not bring this event up in the discussion that followed. I was too preoccupied with the thought that I really was capable of mustering up enough aggression to take a human life. I now completely understood I actually could do what I was being trained to do.

———•———

In the days that followed I was troubled by many thoughts. *Where did this capacity to kill come from? Did it exist somewhere beyond what they were teaching us, something they were adept enough to bring it to the surface? Was it some kind of primordial experience or fear passed down in the gray matter or dormant in some as yet unknown gene? Was it something driving us to remember, re-trigger, re-enact some inbred survival instinct? War, after all, is said to be an "institution." It's been around since the dawn of humanity. I didn't* know the answers then and I still don't; but I finally realized that the ability to take human life is there, deep inside me, perhaps inside all of us.

I once heard it said we must beware of the beast that lurks within. That day, I became keenly aware of this dark spirit. For a split second, I found I wanted to roll with it, like a drunk who was a fast friend with a bottle; it was that easy to become a disciple of violence.

This event made me aware I was now fully re-socialized, trained, and capable of taking life. This is what I had come to. This was the level of success they were having. Everything I learned previously at school and in church had almost been wallpapered over. More than ever, I knew I would have to be on guard to prevent the resurrection of the homicidal beast lurking within. It is a disturbing realization, still shocking some five decades later.

Twenty-Third

——◆•◆——

Sound of Silence

Music is the squeaking of the door of heaven …
I hear it squeaking as it opens to me.

Jalal ad-Din Rumi

Sundays during Advanced Infantry Training (AIT) were essentially real days off for both trainees and most Cadre. The training units operated with a skeleton crew. There was, of course, reveille formation and a trip to the mess hall for breakfast. As I recall, there was not much physical training—perhaps some running before breakfast, but little training. After that, we were pretty much left alone.

Things were refreshingly laid-back, especially on those occasions when guys could get a weekend pass. But there were limits on travel. We could go only so many miles until reaching a "no-go" zone. During AIT, that was not too far; and there was not a whole heck of a lot in the Fort Polk area. But, for quick visits, we could always catch a bus and head to Shreveport.

Shreveport, Louisiana, was a relatively short ride from Fort Polk. One could make the trip on a leave weekend or for several hours on a Sunday. Tired and non-descript, Shreveport seemed a bit larger than GI-towns like Wrightsville, New Jersey. The Shreveport locals knew their retail clientele often came from the base, so a familiar collection of tattoo parlors, Bible stores, and jewelers catered to the needs, emotions, and impulse-buying of anxious troops.

Some Sundays I would grab an early bus to Shreveport and head for the local United Service Organization (USO). It was always open by the time I got there. The USO was in an old retail storefront—complete with a full-length glass display window. For many others, and me, the USO was a welcome oasis available during dark and difficult times. It offered several relaxing or recreational opportunities for drop-ins. There was always coffee, tea, juice, and some snacks, which were often homemade. Sometimes a few of the local girls came in, put on some current music and danced with some of the guys. I have to say I was impressed with the local community's commitment to the USO; folks would volunteer their time to reach out to a group of guys involved in what had already become a divisive and unpopular war.

—•—

But dancing, billiards, or ping pong was not why I was there. That was not my thing, but there were comfy chairs, books, newspapers, magazines, puzzles, and odds-and-ends for guys to enjoy. I came there to get away from it all—for isolation, escape, and especially the music.

There were several popular vinyl albums at the USO, including a few Simon and Garfunkel releases. I always chose *Parsley,*

Sage, Rosemary and Thyme. It was gentle, beautifully poetic, melodic, with tight harmonies and popular, contemporary lyrics. When I went there, I never played anything else.

This USO featured three old-fashioned wooden listening booths, each about the size of a phone booth. Those days, listening booths might be found in most music stores, large or small, selling 45s or albums. These booths allowed potential buyers to check out the tunes before deciding whether to make a purchase.

Usually one of the dark, compact, yet comfortable booths at the USO would be vacant. When I closed the door, I was in my own cozy cocoon. There was a tiny window on the door, a small light inside the booth, and just enough space to sit and spin the disc. I'd grab a drink and a snack and pick up the Simon and Garfunkel album. I'd put the disc on the turntable and pull on the headset. Soon, the music would surround me with the dulcet and prophetic sounds of the time, sometimes angry, often frustrated. It caught the sexual and political laments of disaffected, pining youth... the voices of a generation in deep personal and political pain.

Most of the songs from *Parsley, Sage, Rosemary and Thyme* spoke to the things I was thinking, worrying about, witnessing, or experiencing. I would get lost in lyric and sound, moved in some fashion with each spin of the record. Bits and pieces haunted me as they sang:

- "My life is made of patterns that can scarcely be controlled."
- "My thoughts are scattered and they're cloudy."
- "Like emptiness and harmony, I need someone to comfort me... I wish I was homeward bound..."
- "Slow down, you move too fast."

- "Like a poem poorly written, we are verses out of rhythm, couplets out of rhyme..."
- "Yes, we speak of things that matter with words that must be said."
- "I'm blinded by the light of God and truth and right, and I wander through the night without direction..."
- "I heard the cathedral bells tripping down the alley ways."
- "I been Norman Mailer'd, Maxwell Taylor'd. I been John O'Hara'd, McNamara'd..."
- "...I must be what I must be and face tomorrow."

Then the album's final cut, "7 0'Clock News/Silent Night," would jolt me back to reality. This selection featured a two-part harmony of the traditional hymn "Silent Night" overlaid by an infuriating newscast of current events:

- "...the House Committee on Un-American activities continued its probe into anti-Vietnam war protests. Demonstrators were forcibly evicted from the hearings when they began chanting antiwar slogans..."
- "...Former Vice-President Richard Nixon says that unless there is a substantial increase in the present war effort in Vietnam, the U.S. should look forward to five more years of war...Nixon also said opposition to the war in this country is the greatest single weapon working against the U.S."

That man, Nixon, would soon be elected President of the United States on the promise he had a so-called "secret plan" to end the war. The nation believed him. I sure wanted to.

Those days, I sat in the USO and listened, turning the record over and savoring it again and again. I can't say I paid much attention to whether others were waiting to get into one of the booths, as I was caught up in it and taken out of myself. I loved being enveloped in the enclosed space, smothered by sound pouring out from the headset. If music is the voice of God, I look back and imagine it was the divine trying to crack through, trying to impress the message of resistance into me, perhaps trying to say, "Can't you see you are not alone with your beliefs?"

But I was not consciously hearing in that way. Still, the music touched me even as I wished I could write something as beautiful. But for now, this was enough. This was a gift I needed, accepted, and cherished during every visit.

I just sat quietly and listened—something akin to a silent meditation, to becoming one with the music. It was something known and experienced by holy people who had come before, many from the East from the time of the Buddha. But who thought of it that way? It just felt good; it was an escape; it was fulfilling.

I distanced myself there, shutting out this ragged little town, the base, the training, the raw and ever-present reality and the contradiction of it all. Little did I know this was the beginning of an on-going desire for escape and isolation. A lifelong pattern. A resistance legacy born of an atypical military experience.

Twenty-Fourth

— • —

Busted

Do not wander far and wide but return into yourself.
Deep within us there dwells the truth.

Augustine of Hippo

After visiting the USO, I headed further downtown. There sat a place called the Tiger Inn, a local watering hole, most likely one of many. This one was close enough to the bus station, so why not?

The owners of the Tiger Inn had painted the outside of the place in cheesy, vertical white and orange tiger stripes. Totally outrageous. It stood out in all its tacky glory among the otherwise drab and tired shops in Shreveport. But it sure looked like an oasis and, for me, it *was* one.

Tiger Inn was always very quiet and relatively empty for a mid-Sunday afternoon. Just like in many bars, at least one guy sat there with a true thousand-yard stare; one of those guys you really did not want to approach as he sat there coming to grips with whatever anchored him to his painful, solitary seat. The dimmed lights shining on those who dwelt in darkness, those lurking in the shadow of death, and those looking for some sort of peace. Combat experience or not, GI or civilian, I learned that many complicated events can send one into this distant stare. For me it was by obsessing over troubles when ordering Jax beer—a cheap enough local favorite, but not as cheap as at the PX.

After a couple of Jax, I too would begin to stare into the distance, straight through the neon bracketed mirror on the opposite side of the bar. Entering that chemically induced stillness beyond the looking glass, heading to another empty place; knowing with that look in my eye, no man would dare approach.

The USO and the Tiger Inn became my favorite haunts in Shreveport. Eventually, it was time to head back to the base, grab a woozy nap on the bus, and get to the business of writing home, shining brass and boots, or doing the laundry; all the while trying to stay out of trouble.

———•———

On those relatively laid-back Sundays, guys might go to chapel, do some reading, write home, or visit the PX. One Sunday, after arriving back from Shreveport, I stuffed a duffle bag and pillowcase with my sweaty, filthy clothes, stopped by the PX to pick up a couple more sixteen-ounce cans of Jax beer, and headed off for the laundromat.

Well, you know the drill. I put the soap and the clothes in, waited around, did a little reading, drank a little beer, moved clothes from washer to dryer and popped them out. Before long everything was clean, nicely folded, fresh and ready to go. I was especially careful with the fatigue shirts and pants. They were cotton, so if you got them out of the dryer quickly you could fold them nicely and not get them all wrinkled. It was not easy to find the time, or the iron, to starch and press these things, but my method usually prevented me from being subjected to the DI's periodic wrath, even if they were not pressed.

At this point, deep into the second can of Jax, I was feeling a lot less pain about the frustrations of the week, the exhaustion I felt, the worries I had about my situation, and the correctness of what I was doing. All this kind of washed off me as I went with the warm, chemical glow building up inside. I packed all my stuff and headed back to the barracks.

I cannot be sure if the Military Police also had a skeleton crew on weekends. Possibly not; they had a lot to do. For example, they policed the entrances to the base and regularly drove around to keep an eye on things. They would monitor PX commissaries and the NCO and enlisted men's clubs looking for dress code violations and bad behavior. On occasion, they might deal with a dispute or break up a fight.

When walking on base, troops were expected to salute any officer's car that came in their direction. These could be army-issued or personal vehicles, recognizable by a small flag placed near one of the side mirrors. Troops were supposed to give a salute regardless of who was driving the car—whether officer or family member. That led to some interesting and comic moments when the driver happened to be the officer's spouse or teenage child. Essentially, they laughed at you, especially the teens. If a guy neglected to salute, he might expect to be dressed down by an observant MP. Or, more likely, an offended officer who was driving would screech to a halt, pile out of the car, and scream at the unfortunate troop for not following protocol.

Saluting vehicles struck me as a rather pathetic and useless act, but I learned early on to go through the motions, even if they were half-hearted and limp.

This also seemed to be true for some guys just back from Vietnam who reacted negatively to a lot of the standard operating procedures. They told us about relaxed military discipline and how things were different in Southeast Asia, claiming they did not salute when in the field and often elsewhere. Now, back home and anxious for discharge, these grunts said they could not be bothered with formalities.

According to the vets, the Vietcong and the North Vietnamese Army always took aim at anyone with bars-and-stars insignia—whether the rank was metal or more safely blacked out. In either case, a salute always identified an officer to enemy surveillance. Radiomen and medics were also prime targets, regardless of rank. Thus, blackened insignia for officers and grunts and not saluting anyone became acceptable deviations from standard protocol.

Saluting officers, however, was mandated and considered a big deal stateside and on other relatively safe military bases. So, like most other guys, I gave the brass the benefit of the doubt on saluting cars. Virtually all of us reasoned rank called for this demonstration of respect, and many trainees thought saluting cars was a way for the brass to teach people to be alert and aware of surroundings at all times.

———•———

This day I was heading back to the barracks feeling mellow; I was down to the last few swallows of my warm Jax beer, now concealed inside one of those ubiquitous brown paper bags.

From out of nowhere an MP drove up, pulled right in front of me, and frantically beckoned me to stop. He burst out of the car looking pretty angry. It was clear, on this quiet Sunday afternoon, this was a place he really did not want to be. But there he was; there I was; and he decided we would be there together. He screamed, "What the hell are you doing?" Feeling more than a bit harassed, I replied I was coming back from the laundromat. This, of course, was not the answer he was seeking. In a voice both angry and laced with expletives he screamed, "That's not what I'm talking about you f-ing dope, what the hell do you have in the paper bag!" I reached in and pulled out the long, now almost empty, sixteen ounce can of Jax. He screams, "Get rid of that!" I quickly looked around; there was no trash can. I'm thinking, *was he trying to trick me into littering or was he just being a jerk*?

Okay, I'm a twenty-year-old kid experiencing a bit of a buzz, and I'm now copping an attitude. I'm thinking, hey this thing cost me fifteen cents (we were paid a total of $98 per month before deductions). "Sure, I'll get rid of it."

What happened next was a conscious decision, even if it was one made under the influence of a couple of beers. In one of those moments where hope triumphs over knowledge, I took the can and quaffed it down. For a second, I thought this would appease him, he would laugh it off in this heat and give me a ride back to the barracks. Wrong. Instead, he got livid and came at me with everything in his verbal arsenal. It was colorful and very impressive. If words were fireworks, he would be the Fourth of July. All I could do was tell myself, "Oops, I guess I shouldn't have done that…."

I cannot remember if he put me in handcuffs, but I do recall he had me drop the laundry, which he picked up and carelessly threw into the back of the patrol car. I guessed it was going to be tough to fake being "Strack" this week; just about everything I was trying to keep fresh was now akimbo.

I did get the ride, but not to my training unit. Instead, we drove to the local MP headquarters where we entered with great seriousness and no little fanfare. My custodian put on a small show for the desk Sergeant while summarizing his case. The desk Sergeant did not ask me any questions, nor did we engage in any words or confrontation. Still, he ordered the arresting officer to lock me up.

My lock-up was a ceiling-to-floor chain link fence with a locked gate featuring a wrestling mat or something similar on the floor. A cage. Overreacting and feeling a bit forlorn, I imagined myself sitting in Poe's story "The Cask of Amontillado" watching the bricks and mortar seal me in. Thankfully, this was not a cement cell with a steel door; the "cell" was clearly just a temporary placement.

The desk Sergeant picked up the phone to call my training unit. He wanted to let them know they had me and to ask for the Company Commander. He clearly wanted to turn me in for a potential Article 15 (administrative punishment for low-level infractions). In any case, he wanted to get me the hell out of there and did not want to do the paperwork, especially on a hot and sleepy Sunday afternoon. But, as on most Sundays in the training unit, the Company Commander and his key lieutenants were nowhere to be found. Nor was there a Sergeant in charge; just some lowly trainee, stuck on office duty. Nobody was there with enough juice to decide what to do with a notorious criminal like me.

I sat there locked up for a while, coming down from a bit of a buzz and not completely understanding what was going on.

Relatively inexperienced and now obsessed, I pondered how one could get arrested and detained for such a simple act. I was anxious and wondered about what was going to happen next. After a while I fell asleep for what turned out to be a short nap.

Soon, someone from my training company called and told my jailers to let me out. I was pretty much coming down from the Jax by then, perhaps a bit woozy from short sleep and with a slight hangover. I took my two jumbled bags of laundry and headed out the door.

It was now the early evening on a hot, humid, Louisiana night. I still had to deal with the repercussions of what the Company Commander might say and do. For now, I was sitting on my pity-pot, balancing frustration over my laundry, having been arrested, and the need to get back to my unit. I trudged along feeling disappointed in myself, angry and confused, trying to put the afternoon's events behind me...totally unaware the day's adventure was just beginning.

Twenty-Fifth

———◆●◆———

Be Still and Know...

Rock-n-roll music, in the end,
is a source of religious and mystical power.

Bruce Springsteen

Cresting one last hill on my way back to the barracks, I stood in the dense Louisiana humidity, under a brilliant red sky among the pale to dark gray clouds suspended over the facilities. *Just another relaxed, late Sunday afternoon on the base*, I thought to myself. There were no people to be seen walking around the barracks. Just me under an inspirational, assertive sky with thick, dirt-sweet wet air and serene quiet. I set the laundry bags down and stood there taking in this implausible scene.

Just then, the mesmerizing extended version of Creedence Clearwater Revival's song *Suzie Q* came blasting out of some unknown window. It reverberated off the buildings and filled the entire area with sound. Truth be told, the song itself had a trite and silly set of lyrics seemingly about one man's total adoration for a woman. But this version captivated audiences with its emphasis on the production and sound. The pleading, hungry, swamp-rock voice of John Fogerty, and the band's guitar riffs, hypnotic beats, distortions and feedback grabbed me and drew me in.

I stood there amazed at the audacity of some anonymous trainee bold enough to pump up the volume. This type of thing could only be pulled-off when no officers or other Cadre were around. But there it was: the heat, the humidity, the salty sweat-soaked fatigue shirt, the anger, the sadness, the sky, the sound… and me. Me, the guy who had just spent time in a military cage. Me, the guy afraid of going to prison. Me, realizing—you know what? I had just been in jail for the crime of drinking a beer in a bag while carrying laundry. A simple, silly thing—just like the song—meaningless in the scheme of things.

━ • ━

In truth, I had only been locked up for a relatively short time, a few hours at most. And yet, I could not help thinking about the future. *What would it be like to be incarcerated for one full day? For a couple of days, a week, a month, a year, or more? What kinds of activities might exist in jail? Reading? Some kind of work? And what about the stigma of imprisonment, how does one get past it? As unfair as it seemed, was going to prison for war resistance so implausible? After all, Henry David Thoreau and Martin Luther King, Jr. went to jail for their beliefs.* I began to wonder if what previously seemed so fantastic had now acquired some sense of possibility.

Strangely, standing there looking down on the barracks I felt freer than ever. Here, in this place, there were no weapons around. No sounds of the firing-line, or of screaming, anxious, often fearful boys. Here in the heat, in the setting sun, sur-rounded by the music of Creedence Clearwater Revival and God's gracious gifts.

Too tired to think about all this, I hung my head and closed my eyes. In the moment it seemed the normal thing to do. It felt inexplicably comfortable and familiar, as if I were following some primordial draw into the sea, wrapped in the all-encompassing peace and healing power of the living ocean; surrounded, in silence, within the roaring waves. It held me up, assaulted all my senses, touched me in a way that seemed all too soothing and complicated to ponder. Like being in a space found somewhere between reality and dreams.

All this came crashing in, gently filling my mind and body. Exultant, confused, and even a bit scared, I could not take it, it was too overwhelming. I felt an intense need to get back in control. And then, just like that, it came to me—"*You will not be going to prison.*" Unbeknownst to me, I had experienced what has been called an "invisible thought," a knowing, a revelation: I would not be going to prison. My eyes sprung open as once again I saw, heard, felt, tasted, and was aware of all the material things around me.

A bit weak-kneed, I swayed in stunned disbelief. Yet I never doubted or challenged this thought. I just knew it, even if I con-tinued to have doubts about the future, even though everything I was previously thinking and doing indicated events would turn out differently.

I was vaguely aware a window of fear, one opened in my earliest days, had been slammed shut—the one that beckons all good little Catholic kids to "walk the straight and narrow" and to "keep our noses clean." But this day I had been caught, detained, and put in a cage. Not a prison, of course, but a jail nevertheless. A taste of what losing my freedom was like and what usually happens when one breaks the law.

Back then, I was not wise enough to understand when one of life's windows closes another just might crack open. That day, I slowly and hesitantly began to pry this new window open. Yet at the time, I did not think about my unknown future in this way.

Truthfully, I cannot say I was a completely changed young man. Indeed, all things human beckoned me to be logical and realistic. There was so much more yet to learn, although the boy in me insisted I knew enough. It was as if I had been dropped on a slackline desperately trying to gain my balance. There I was, oscillating somewhere between command and conscience, the physical and the unphysical.

—•—

By now, Creedence had rocked-on for over eight minutes, then suddenly it was gone, and all fell quiet once again. Total silence. Everything else was there but the sound. I wiped my brow with my sweat-stained sleeve, picked up the laundry, and headed down to the barracks.

Postscript: I never heard another thing about being arrested and detained; it was as if it never happened.

Twenty-Sixth

———— • ————

Daily Bread

A single sunbeam is enough to drive away many shadows.

Francis of Assisi

O ver the next several days, I continued to revisit the events of that Sunday. I wondered if I could stay strong and continue to be heard. Or if I would give up the fight, get with the program, and let them do with me what they wanted?

As I struggled with this, I decided not to talk about that mystifying experience with anyone, not the folks in the army who were to decide my fate, not my wife, not my future children, not other GIs, veterans, not any priest, peace activist, or helper. Who would want to listen to me after hearing such a tale? I wanted to be taken seriously and not dismissed as some pie-in-the-sky hippie. I decided it was better to keep it all to myself.

Very quickly, the scripted demands of daily Advanced Infantry Training (AIT) kept me from giving all this deeper thought. I needed a diversion, and I was about to get one.

Kitchen Patrol was nonstop, early morning to late evening; but again, for me it was a wonderfully welcome reprieve and good work. At minimum, the twelve-hour KP shifts relieved us from training and other mundane details of army life. Most of the trainees hated KP and tried to avoid it; but I enjoyed working in a kitchen. This was no accident; for on those days, I was in my element. Back in the world, I managed the nightshift of an independent fast-food restaurant. It was what I did at that time in my life. I liked the feel of it, the hectic pace, the challenge, the camaraderie, the teamwork, and the feelings of accomplishment as we got hot food out to hungry customers.

KP assignment meant doing all the grunt-work, cleaning, mopping, taking orders from cooks, etc. I accepted this and did not have a problem with any of it, though most did. I liked backing up the cooks and bakers, doing various odd jobs like getting the kitchen and serving area ready, feeding the seemingly never-ending line of hungry, often filthy troops, and doing the chores related to clean up. It was an act of *Diakonia* in its own way: service to others. Back in the world, you even got paid for it!

Once on bivouac after a particularly rough day of Survival Skills Training, we were instructed to cook dinner out in the boonies.

This time, there were no field stoves or cooks on site. Instead, firewood was provided and small units of five or six men went to work building fires at each campsite. The task was to cook chicken and heat precooked rice for dinner. No instruction or guidance was given. No one was issued any cooking utensils beyond their mess kits.

Our Platoon Sergeant ordered me to help hand out dinner supplies from the back of a 2½ ton truck. Getting pulled away from my buddies at our campsite seemed like bad duty to me at the time, but it turned out to be a very fortuitous event. My job was to hand out food while the rest of the men built fires and started to cook their meals. Each troop received a piece of raw chicken, one precooked rice ball in aluminum foil, and a slice or two of bread. Sensing an opportunity, I grabbed a roll of aluminum foil and an extra-large loaf of bread and stashed them in my knapsack.

For the most part, these were inexperienced, hungry teenagers straight from asphalt and concrete streets. These troops were exhausted and wanted to eat, as quickly as possible. Some had gone camping at some point in their life; most had not. Virtually none had ever prepared anything other than toast and Kool Aid.

I noticed many fires blazed too hot. Several guys skewered chicken with the small fork from our mess kits, or with a large stick dangling the meat over the roaring flames; fingers were getting burnt and some wooden skewers caught fire. A lot of the chicken began to look like large, overly blackened marshmallows. Picture too, precooked aluminum balls of rice thrown directly into the base of the fire; think burnt and crusted rice stuck to the interior of aluminum foil.

I headed back to my assigned unit after distributing food and quickly encouraged the guys to stand down and listen up. I told them to tamp down the blazing fire and showed them how best to cook the chicken and heat the rice. I had them wrap the chicken in the purloined aluminum foil and set it close to, but not into, the fire, explaining the meat would cook in its juices and if they flipped it frequently it would not burn to a crisp. It took longer, but we ended up with a decent meal, one including as much bread as we could eat. Manna gathered for the ravenous masses. Nothing near Tolkien's "Elfin Bread," but it was the filling, physical bread of life. We sat in contentment. In communion.

Soon guys relaxed, settled in to share stories, and inevitably began debating the war. Some were excited about Richard Nixon running for president with his self-proclaimed "secret plan" to end the war. Some thought his opponent, Senator Hubert Humphrey, was too weak and not a viable candidate. Some believed by voting for Nixon this conflict would soon come to an end and we would not be shipped to Vietnam. Many civilians shared this belief, enough to elect Nixon in November of 1968.

None of us grunts suspected Nixon's "secret plan" would result in many more American casualties and increased death and destruction for the Vietnamese. The bottom line was we knew most of us around our campfire would be ordered to Nam. Our vote for, and trust in, the "secret plan" would not matter. Our belief in it proved to be just another youthful triumph of hope over experience.

It was almost twilight; we were laidback and thought the day was done. Surely we would soon board trucks, head back to our barracks, and get some rest. Suddenly, our contentment was interrupted by the frantic demands of the Cadre urging us to hurry up, dose the fires, grab gear, form up, and head toward some nearby bleachers. The Survival Skills cooking lesson was over. The real reason for being out on this bivouac was soon to come.

Twenty-Seventh

---•---

Bloodlust

He fixed his eyes on the bloody pastime,
unwittingly drinking in the madness.

Augustine of Hippo

The Cadre went about the business of lighting several large bonfires around the perimeter as we poured onto the bleachers. Suddenly, a Drill Instructor (DI) appeared carrying a chicken in his arms. He reminded the trainees there would be no field kitchens available in certain situations, like in combat areas or when we were lost or cut off from a base. Therefore, we should not expect to receive precut chicken as we experienced earlier in the evening. Obviously, we needed to learn how to feed ourselves under difficult circumstances. In these situations, troops would have to forage or steal animals and be able to prepare them for cooking. Therefore, this night we would be taught how to dispatch a chicken and clean it out.

Specifically, tonight we would learn how to yank the head off a live chicken. As a nervous murmur arose from the crowd, the DI mimicked how this would be done. To demonstrate, he grasped the chicken under his arm and pretended to snap and twist the head off the bird. Many trainees looked back and forth at each other in wonder and fascination as a nervous laughter now spilled from the crowd.

But there was more to come. The DI announced he was not about to do this himself but would choose some poor grunt to complete this duty. Of course, he had someone in mind before we even got there. That someone was a guy we will call Wagner. He was a meek and sensitive fellow who often struggled with many of the things we were asked to do. He was sensitive and quiet, but not effeminate as some guys clearly were.

Wagner was kindhearted, easily upset, uncomfortable with the training, and very likely to be picked on, ridiculed, and otherwise abused by some members of the Cadre and his peers. He reminded me of the kid who sits alone in the school lunchroom terrified at the thought of interacting with others, an easy mark for bullies.

Wagner was shocked when called on to perform this ritual. But many of those in our company roared in delight. Looking around nervously, he slowly descended the bleachers in disbelief and trepidation. Wagner then recoiled as the DI stuffed the chicken into his hands. He was clearly hesitant and squeamish as he peered out into the crowd to look for someone, anyone, who could feel his pain and perhaps offer a supportive nod or look that might offer strength and support. I was too far away for him to see, but I was one of those guys who empathized with him and felt the same anger and disgust toward that DI.

The night sky gave way to a growing conflagration casting eerie shadows and a warm, menacing orange-red glow over the scene. The Cadre were waving their arms and frantically trying to pump up the crowd, much like a cheerleader does at a high school pep rally. But this was different. Various screams of approval and chants arose from the scrum: "Do it!" "Waste it!" "Kill it!" Most were accompanied by assorted expletives to underscore the bloodlust, seal the animal's fate, and perhaps appease their own curiosity.

Poor Wagner. Of all the grunts in this company, there he stood with his soft, now frightened and wild eyes. Eyes looking for escape, for someone else to do this, for some sort of human understanding. It was cold fear at minimum. Terror at worst. He was now forced to do something totally foreign to his makeup. But that was the idea; he was chosen on purpose. Wagner stood there, center-stage, illuminated against the fiery background with his manhood and his need to be accepted as one of the guys once again on the line. Wagner, just another maggot forced to satisfy the incessant demands of those appointed to usurp our civilian ways, strengthen our resolve to kill, and, as they claimed, get us back home alive and in one piece.

This would be the first time most of us witnessed something being killed. On another occasion, we watched in awe as an M-16 magazine was emptied into a cinder block. In a split-second it was turned into gravel and dust amid the "Oohs" and "Aahs" of the trainees. It did not take much imagination to understand what a human body would look like if subjected to automatic firepower—flesh would fly and body parts tear off as a bloody mist rained down on the remains. But tonight was different; it was hands-on, personal, deadly. Not a drop of imagination was needed.

——•——

I watched Wagner take the bird from the DI's hands, much like a first-time father would awkwardly reach for a baby. You could see he would rather cuddle the bird or toss it on the ground perhaps hoping it—and he—could run away. But this would not happen. The blood lust from the crowd reached a fevered din amid the now blazing night sky. The guys shrieked, something like spectators at an ancient coliseum who sought amusement by watching a prisoner or gladiator dispatched.

Once again, the DI barked instructions as Wagner violently twisted the head of the bird, trying to tear it off. Wounded, desperate for escape, its head hanging to one side, the bird did not die. Wagner, now psychically wounded, ridiculed, and humiliated, also had enough. He thrust the dying animal back into the hands of the laughing DI and stepped back.

The Drill Instructor grabbed the bird, pushed Wagner out of the way, ripped the head off its body, and threw it to the ground. Now in death throes, and much to the delight and excitement of the crowd, the headless animal scurried around in circles until it collapsed into stillness, blood oozing from its headless neck. Meanwhile Wagner, pale, stunned, and falling back, was a whimpering mass of shock and embarrassment. Head down, exiting stage right, he reached out for some sort of support as he grasped the handrail on the bleachers while the fires roared behind him. His quivering shadow danced wildly in front of the audience. I watched it in shock, anger, and sorrow.

It was finished. Or so the screaming horde imagined. But this was only the opening act. The DI picked up the bleeding bird, thrust his fingers into the leaking neck and began flicking blood over the amazed and excited troops. Walking crisply in front of the crowd, he splashed blood on our faces, our uniforms, our heads; a baptism of blood sanctified by flame. An initiation into the club: to taste, to see, to kill.

And, "click," there it was. This is what we do. This is what we are all about. We were infantry soldiers.

I sat there in total amazement. I knew what I was seeing, just what this ceremony was all about. It was not so much concerned with preparing animals for dinner. It was about the fires of war and operating within them, about burning and killing, about carrying on while covered in your own gore or with the blood of others. It was a preparation for hell on earth. Indeed, this deadly vignette, with its fire, flame, and blood was in and of itself an experience of hell on earth. Nevertheless, this was just the first act in the deadly drama that lie ahead. Soon, there would be another show, the ritual reception of orders—infantry status confirmed with all too many heading off to what many of us suspected, and history affirms, was mission impossible in Vietnam.

Years later, I almost jumped out of my seat at the very end of the film *Full Metal Jacket* when the troops, some of whom had witnessed their buddies shot by a sniper, closed in on their adversary. In the film, there was at least one conflicted GI; a character who wore a peace sign on his helmet—the so-called, "Footprint of the American Chicken"—his doubts about the war and what he was doing boldly displayed on his head. He, like Wagner, suffered the same doubts about taking a life, not of a chicken, but of a captured and wounded VC sniper. Ultimately, he too, would take matters into his own hands; he would do what he was trained to do.

Then, in the movie's final scene, his platoon marched out of the town with the radiant flames of the burning city in hellish relief. For cadence they chanted "M-I-C-K-E-Y M-O-U-S-E", the *Mickey Mouse Club* song we all learned as children. The burning, the killing, the destruction was over. For them, and for so many of us, this war was "Mickey Mouse." Empty, futile, pointless. For all too many, a mission accomplished, even if some guys said "it don't mean nothin."

———•———

On the ride back to our dorms, I gave myself a good talking to. What was I thinking? Why did I imagine anyone involved in processing a war—Selective Service or military—cared about what I believed? Beliefs could be handled, worked around, ignored. Mine sure were. That night more pieces of my personal puzzle fell into place. I knew I had seen, heard, and learned enough to convince me what I was doing was wrong. It was undeniably clear what we were expected to do as soldiers. I now knew too many ways to unleash my human animal. I was slowly coming to understand belief without action was inadequate. Talking and reasoning was not enough. I had to walk the talk. It was time to take a different path, to fight a different fight, unarmed and unafraid. To step onto the thin ice and accept the consequences.

Once again, my head was swimming. *What was I going to do? Was I ready for prison and a dishonorable discharge? Should I just give up and join those headed for Canada? Did I have enough strength to stand up to the system? Who was out there who could help—a chaplain, a peace group, other antiwar GIs? Was it up to those of us who were locked into this system to oppose the war? Per-haps even to try to stop it? Was it time for me to join the resistance?*

I did not have answers, but I felt ready to stand up and find out. This I did know: many civilians, including clergy and some politicians had done their best but had not been able to end the war. I also knew that more and more GIs and veterans were act-ing out, speaking up, and organizing against the war. Mostly, I understood my Advanced Infantry Training was coming to an end and—despite future orders—somehow, someway, I would not allow myself to be shipped to Vietnam. Period.

Twenty-Eighth

— • —

Confirmation

I was standing with my back to the light,
so that the things that should be illuminated were in shadow,
even though they were in front of my face.

Augustine of Hippo

Graduation day arrived on 5 November 1968. That morning, we formed ranks in a field as the Commanding Officer barked out orders sending us to our next duty stations. So many guys hoped for assignments to a safe place like Germany; but only a handful would be called to go there. I noticed many men stood as if in prayer with heads bowed, sometimes slouching in a ragged and uncaring approximation of parade rest.

The Commanding Officer barked out each name, alphabetically citing the transport station with his voice amplified over and over with the final pronouncement, "Vietnam," "Vietnam," "Vietnam!" Some guys moaned softly, their futures sealed and uncertain. When he reached my name, he again screamed, "Fort

Lewis, Washington, 8 November, for transport to Vietnam, 30 November 1968." I held my head high knowing moral outrage, previous religious schooling, and logical debate with the power structure would never get us out of this. I was ready for the fight back, whatever that meant.

———•———

In the pinelands of New Jersey and in the woodlands and plains of Louisiana, I learned to march and to grunt, to attack and defend, to escape and to survive, and to shoot to kill. All in the service of a war many of us considered immoral and illegal. All this training was an attempt to get me to step into a way of being that did not fit me…much like toughened dough unsuited for a cookie cutter. But others proudly chose this life and this war. For many it became a good-enough fit, even if most had to be pounded into the mold. Their cloudy futures were sealed in a distant jungle, a place where, as required, you could totally lose control of yourself, where war was deemed glorious and all the things done were cause for acclaim. But I had finally seen enough.

PART IV

——•——

Hell No!

I was done with the lies about the war and my own personal doubts and compromises. I was done blowing in the wind and letting events shape me. As tempting as other choices seemed, I still would not run, leave the country, or hide out in the hinterlands of America. I decided the army could either discharge or court martial me; but they would not get me to kill in that war. It was crunch time. Time to take a stronger stand. I was ready to pick myself up, let my actions speak louder than words, and see just what I was made of.

I knew what I was not going to do, but I did not have a plan. I did not know how to proceed and decided to get the help I needed to set things into motion. Before I headed west, I did some research, picked up the phone, and called the Catholic Peace Fellowship in New York City.

Twenty-Ninth

—●—

Fort Lewis

You can't go back and change the beginning,
but you can start where you are and change the ending.

C. S. Lewis

We were ordered to arrive at the Fort Lewis Overseas
Replacement Center no later than November 30, 1968,
to prepare for shipment to Vietnam in early December. Some
guys decided to take a leave before flying west; others, like
myself, hung around Fort Polk and flew out to Fort Lewis near
Tacoma, Washington, toward the end of the month. It was the
last time I saw any of the guys I trained with at Fort Polk.

I arrived a few days early and was billeted in what was called
a "Holding Company" along with others who were shipping to,
or coming back from, Vietnam. I noticed some of the guys coming back were pretty edgy and were clearly dog tired. For a night
or two, I slept across from a returnee who stayed to himself,
smoking and sleeping. Once his Zippo lighter crashed to the

floor and he awoke in a start, wild-eyed and screaming, thinking he was under attack. At that time, we did not have a name for this kind of nocturnal or any other "startle reactions," what we now call "Post-Traumatic Stress Disorder (PTSD). But we both knew he was in for a heck of a time adjusting to being back in the world.

The Catholic Peace Fellowship referred me to an attorney in Seattle for help with my situation. After settling into the Holding Company and securing my gear, I gave the lawyer a call to set up an appointment. I got a pass and headed off to Seattle for a couple of days surrounding Thanksgiving.

———•———

Charles H. W. Talbot, Esq. (aka Chas) maintained an office in the gray-granite, eight-story Central Building on Third Street in downtown Seattle. I was led into an office stacked with law books strewn on shelves, chairs, and the floor. A jumble of open books, legal briefs, and papers littered the desk. The place looked like a law school library hit by a tornado.

Chas was short, comfortably dressed in white shirt and casual slacks and wearing his signature bowtie. My mind's eye remembers him in suspenders, but I cannot be sure. In any case, he was not a poster boy for the stereotypical lawyer decked out in a business suit. Welcoming, enthusiastic, and positive, he was glad to hear me out and offer personal insights and legal advice.

He advised me to return to the base, visit my Company Commander, and immediately file for a discharge on the basis of conscientious objection. I was shocked to find out a soldier could do such a thing; no officer who interviewed me ever mentioned this was possible. Chas was not surprised. From his perspective, no officer wanted to deal with the paperwork—or the stigma—of having a trainee discharged for conscientious objection while under his command.

—•—

Chas told me I was a classic case of the guy who seriously considered applying for conscientious objector status from the Selective Service System but for some reason had not. He pointed out that as a civilian, I did not have enough knowledge or experience to follow through. However, the military could grant conscientious objector status to those whose beliefs crystallized as a result of their experiences in the military. He told me one could apply for noncombatant status and remain in the military or could apply for discharge. If approved for noncombatant status, the conscientious objector (C.O.) could be sent for additional training, to another base, or to Vietnam as a noncombatant, perhaps as a clerk. If approved for discharge, the C.O. would immediately be honorably discharged.

On the other hand, Chas said, if a discharge was not approved, I would be back to square one. Then I would have to make a decision to either give up and ship to Vietnam or to confront a court-martial facing up to three years in prison at Fort Leavenworth, Kansas.

As I recall, Chas was also a volunteer American Civil Liberties (ACLU) attorney; so, with a glint in his eye, he also suggested that, depending on the military's response, I might want to consider taking them to court. The idea was to advance the cause of all conscientious objectors by trying to change existing laws under the Uniform Code of Military Justice. In any case, he told me, I had his support and he would be pleased to represent me in all legal matters.

———•———

Chas was twice my age—one of the very few folks over thirty I would believe in for a very long time. I liked Chas and, despite having it drilled into me from a young age to be wary of lawyers (and by all means to stay out of court), I trusted and respected him.

I left the building totally flabbergasted with all I had just learned. But beyond this, I was hopeful and enthused. It was not so much as if the dark night of my soul burst into the daylight but more like the biblical candle was no longer concealed under a wicker basket. The path forward was now dimly lit, I had the help I needed, and I now knew exactly what I had to do.

Thirtieth

━━●━━

Beginning Again

You placed me where I might grow strong again.

Augustine of Hippo

After visiting Chas Talbot, I decided to walk around the historic city of Seattle, staying overnight in a nearby hotel and spending the next day taking in some of the sights. My first impulse was to visit a beach by Elliott Bay. That day the sky was clear in Seattle, a place known to be overcast and rainy. The bright sun lit up the city and radiated a deep blue hue off the waters of Puget Sound. In that part of town, the seascape was far from pristine. Rather, it was punctuated with cargo ships, sailboats, and motor craft. The beach was sparse and crowded with huge maritime piers and intermittent docks for pleasure craft—nature and the economy all sharing space in a mad mix of business and pleasure.

As a frequent visitor to the Jersey Shore, I found it good to simply be by the water, in the place where the sea meets the sky and the earth. And, in this case, the cityscape and the hustle and bustle of marine activity. I sat down on a swatch of sand above the maritime scene, tried not to think about anything, and simply let it all seep in; glad to be on my own, away from my troubles, and truly at ease. I sat there for some time before heading back to town for the evening.

—•—

The next day was Thanksgiving 1968. Like so many other GIs, I was alone and away from family. Loneliness was relatively new for me as I rarely felt that way as a child or teenager; but I sure felt it that day in Seattle. Still, I had a plan and plenty of time on my hands, so I grabbed a street map and headed out. First, I stopped by the famed Pike Place Market with its small shops and kiosks. It was surprisingly busy for a holiday as folks grabbed last-minute essentials for their family gathering. The place was an olfactory and gastronomical wonder, with an amazing array of foodstuffs and other goods for sale—fish, meats, produce, coffee, baked goods, and much more. I could not resist picking up some food for lunch before I continued my tour.

Like most Americans, I was intrigued by the futuristic Seattle Space Needle at the Seattle Center and the monorail that brought you to it. This, of course, had to be experienced. So, I hopped the unmanned, quiet, and amazingly smooth-riding monorail for the short trip to the Needle. I walked around, bought a ticket, and headed up to the observation deck. It was another clear day in the Seattle-Tacoma area and the visibility was superb. The view of the cityscape from this height was humbling; an astonishing demonstration of what humanity had wrought. Even more incredible was the stunning view of what

God had wrought, including the vast forests to the east, where Mount Rainier, although some 100 miles away, towered over the landscape at about 14,400 feet.

By now, I knew I had to pick up the telephone, share this experience, and feign some holiday cheer with my wife, Connie, and other family members back home. Though distant and lonely, I did my best, stayed away from discussing my situation, and shared some love. The calls took the edge off my feelings of being disconnected, even if I was some 3,000 miles away.

By late afternoon my bucket list was completed and I was essentially broke; I headed to the bus station and got a ride back to the base. I knew it would be quiet around Fort Lewis during this holiday weekend. All the better, for now it was time to turn the army's "Do. Don't think," mandate on its head, for I had much to think about, and even more than I could imagine doing.

———•———

On Monday morning, I met with my Company Commander. After exchanging formalities, I was told to sit down and then I got right to the point. I told him I was filing for conscientious objector status and would not be shipping out to Vietnam. His eyes widened and, in a raised and frustrated voice, he shouted, "Oh hell, not again!" He shook his head and demanded to know if I was sure. I responded affirmatively. Clearly frustrated, he sarcastically said, "What will you say to your sons when they ask, "What did you do in the war, Daddy?" I did not take the bait; but as politely as I could I replied something like, "I'm not sure, Sir."

He was clearly upset but was required by army regulations to follow through. Angry and dismissive, he ordered me to make sure I collected all my jungle gear from the quartermaster. That way I would be ready to ship when the paperwork was reviewed and adjudicated. He said that in his experience it was routine for conscientious objector applications to be denied and, once mine was, I would again be issued orders to ship to Vietnam. He made it clear I would either ship out or, if I continue to refuse, he would court martial me for disobeying a direct order.

The Company Commander reviewed the procedures saying I would be given the official conscientious-objector application form from the duty Sergeant, given ten days to answer the questions on the form, and be interviewed by both a chaplain and a psychiatrist. They would send their findings and recommendations to him. The paperwork would then be reviewed by him for his recommendation. My application and all recommendations to deny or approve would be sent to Departmental Headquarters on the base, who would also make their recommendation and send the package to the Department of Defense (DOD) in Washington, DC, for final adjudication.

He said the entire process could take anywhere from a few weeks to several months. He also told me I would be retained in his unit until a decision had been reached by DOD. I was instructed to speak with our duty Sergeant to determine where I would work each day and the type of duty I would perform while waiting for a decision on my application. Finally, before he told me to get out, he said I would be billeted in a Garrison Company with a group of others who were awaiting decisions on various health, hardship, and other reassignments or discharges. I saluted, turned, and went to the orderly room to get my application forms.

I felt great. I had not allowed myself to be intimidated by my Company Commander. I had conquered my fear, stood toe to toe with an officer, stayed the course, and made a stand. It was amazing. I now had ten whole days to write, all the while surrounded by a group of men seeking to be reassigned or discharged for any number of reasons. I could not help but wonder what they were like, if any were antiwar, how I would be received, and if we would get along.

It turns out I was in for quite a surprise. I had not been told the dorm included about a dozen kindred spirits—all conscientious objectors. "Oh hell, not again!" And again.

Oh yeah. Game on.

Thirty-First

——•——

Bay of Pigs

*The bound of human friendship has a sweetness of its own,
binding many souls together as one.*

Augustine of Hippo

After picking up paperwork from the duty sergeant, I went to the quartermaster the next day to secure jungle gear given to those of us with orders to Vietnam. We were issued new camouflage style fatigues and a couple pair of canvas and leather "Jungle Boots," designed for use in moist environments. We were also allowed to rummage through huge boxes of discarded olive-drab fatigues, black leather boots, fatigue caps, and field jackets. These had been cast-off by discharged troops and others who left them behind. Some of them even had the last names and chevrons of the previous owners on the shirts and jackets. Many of them were better than mine, so I used this opportunity to replace faded and torn fatigues and to grab a couple extra field jackets.

Finally, I gathered up my gear, and headed over to the Garrison Company barracks. I found the dorm, unpacked my stuff, and started looking at the application for discharge as a conscientious objector.

To apply as a conscientious objector, you had to provide information requested in DoD 1300.6. It was remarkably similar to the Selective Service Form 150 sent to civilians seeking conscientious objector status. The questions on DoD 1300.6, however, focused on how an applicant's beliefs had developed and gelled *since* entering the service.

I decided to spend the rest of the day trying to set up interviews with a Catholic chaplain and schedule an interview with a shrink. Also, before I started writing, I wanted to scout a typewriter so I could produce a clean, legible document.

In a short time, guys started returning to the barracks from various duties. Others arrived from their job assignments at the end of the day. Some of their jobs were pretty awful, if not vindictive, like shoveling manure or cutting firewood for an officer's residence.

There were about two dozen men housed with me. Some were seeking transfers or reassignments, applying for conscientious objection discharge, or otherwise awaiting further orders. All were welcoming, and it soon became apparent none of these guys felt they belonged in the military. Many of them had already spent some time in the stockade, either for resistance activity or low-level violations of protocol.

The exact number of conscientious objectors in the Garrison Company escapes me, but every single one of these guys had already filed for discharge. Most of us were white; there was one Black, and a Hispanic guy was now housed in the infirmary. We ranged in age from twenty to about twenty-five. We were

Catholics, Protestants, a Jewish-Buddhist, and a freethinker. As I recall, all of us had at least some college and one was headed to medical school.

It was hard to believe we were all in the same barracks. This seemed counter intuitive; that is, I imagined the army would like to keep war resisters and general malcontents away from any sort of support network. The others guys, however, thought the military put us all together so they could keep an eye on us. Of course, we were all wary and distrustful of the brass, but it made sense: The army probably did not want to put those who refused to participate in war with others, filling their heads with all sorts of nonsense about war resistance and nonviolence. In any case, we all understood that beyond the walls of our dormitory this kind of thing was happening anyway. Whatever the reason, the Garrison Company was a welcoming and deeply supportive atmosphere. It was a great relief to be among folks who thought the same way I did.

—•—

I was immediately informed the men had lovingly renamed our barracks the "Bay of Pigs." Historically, this moniker was the codename for a C.I.A-planned Cuban-exile invasion of Cuba in the early 1960s. The goal was to overthrow Fidel Castro's communist regime; but the operation turned out to be a total fiasco. In our case, we did live in a "bay" or dorm inside the Garrison Company barracks. In addition, it was clear few of the brass had any respect for us. Thus, it was a short leap from being called "maggots" in training to embracing the insults and referring to our home at Fort Lewis as a gathering place for "swine."

We supported one another in our individual struggles and talked about the rapidly growing GI antiwar movement and how we might contribute to the resistance. I cannot say I got close to everyone in the barracks. Guys tended to form cliques and several simply and easily gravitated together. For the most part, this was based on temperament, ideology, and experience. Still, we considered everyone in the dorm brothers in the struggle we all confronted. In no time I grew to know and hang out with several of these young men.

———•———

I identified and formed a fellowship with certain guys and we quickly bonded. We shared a deep determination to see this through, often hung out together and supported one another—both on and off the base. I am not hesitant to use the first names of most of these men, as I presented some of their stories previously in *Days of Decision: An Oral History of Conscientious Objectors in the Military During the Vietnam War*. However, I will use pseudonyms for three of them. One was hesitant about going public; I never discussed anonymity with the man in the infirmary; and I lost track of another. For these reasons, I err on the side of confidentiality.

Two of the guys in our clique were older than the rest of us. Rudy had attended three years of medical school, hoped to finish, and eventually would become a doctor in civilian life. Unlike the rest of us, Rudy was a completely cooperative, totally "strack" troop. If Webster's issued a military dictionary, his picture could appear next to this word. Tall, stately, and clean shaven, his fatigues and dress greens were impeccably pressed;

his boots and brass glistened. He did everything by the book. His salutes were sharp and his demeanor respectful; his about-face and military manner were textbook examples of how it was supposed to be done. Humble, dignified, thoughtful, and extremely intelligent, Rudy felt it was a citizen's duty to serve his or her country; but he also believed that a Christian citizen-soldier's duty is to first serve one's conscience. He was willing and able to participate in most things military, but he drew a line when it came to violating his conscience by being shipped to Vietnam.

I believe the brass thought Rudy would crack given his rigorous observance of military protocol. Nevertheless, he made his opposition to the war very clear from his first interaction with military recruiters and reaffirmed his position with subsequent commanders. *Primum non nocere.* "First, do no harm." That was Rudy's mantra.

At age twenty-five, Richard may have been the oldest among us. Mustached like most of us, he was of medium build with the occasional sparkling eyes of a Leprechaun. Educated in philosophy by the Jesuits, he understood irony and absurdity. Deeply knowledgeable, wise beyond his years, and approachable, he was a teacher not confined by the walls of a classroom. Picture your favorite, casual-cool professor with patches on the elbows of a well-worn corduroy jacket. We often sought Richard out; I certainly learned from him and respected his opinions.

Howie was a skilled photographer, an average guy with a sharp intellect, and always quick with a joke. He was a punster and, if you fell into it, the puns would continue for quite some time, even for weeks. He kept us in laughs, and we all shared many good times. Here was a man who fully enjoyed life and approached everything with high expectations. Unlike most young adults I knew, you could see he had a clear view of his civilian future.

Howie identified as a Jewish-Buddhist. One of the Jewish chaplains named him a "Moshe-Buddha"—perhaps one of few gracing the world with their presence. Another officer was flabbergasted when Howie described his belief system. He concluded Buddhism was not a recognized religious philosophy. That officer had absolutely no idea of the ancient Buddhist tradition nor the impact it had on a good portion of the world, including among the people of Vietnam.

Howie found humor, antidotes, and useful contradictions in many of the things we experienced during our time together. Once a group of us went to see the Beatles film, *Yellow Submarine*. There was a creature in the film who sucked everything up. Eventually there was nothing left to devour, so ultimately it sucked itself up. Howie called this the "Sucking Process." That is, it's the tendency for all things evil or unsavory to destroy everything in its path and ultimately destroy itself. At first, he applied this to the U.S. involvement in Vietnam, suggesting militarism was leading us down a path where we must destroy everything as part of a quest that would ultimately lead us to destroy ourselves.

Some of us took Howie's lead. We started applying the concept of the Sucking Process to many aspects of our everyday experiences, like when confronting make-work duty assignments, getting busted for minor infractions, confronting the stockade or a court-martial, or having any number of other difficult life experiences. One guy might ask another guy, "How was your day?" The response would be something like, "Oh man, I was up against the Sucking Process again all day, everything getting swept up around me as if I was falling into a black hole."

Like so many of us, Howie found a particular way to remain true to himself. In his case, he stayed close to his aesthetic by producing fine photographic works. One day we saw a poster encouraging people to enter the base's photography contest. Howie was ecstatic, took some pictures, and developed them at the base photography lab. Pleased with his products, he submitted the art. Some weeks later we learned this conscientious objector, this guy who rejected orders to Vietnam, this guy who might end up in Fort Leavenworth prison, had won the base photography contest. Outstanding! We were proud of him and hysterical about the incongruity of his amazing accomplishment.

Tom was the "anti-Rudy" of the group, a genuine child of the 1960s; a joyous, brave, freethinking soul to be sure. Comfortably disheveled and unassuming, he casually meandered through the system as if he were a visitor from some distant place, as if totally unschooled in army procedures and way beyond most things military. Tom was kind, giving and funny—totally convinced of the absolute absurdity of the war and our own current position.

It seemed like nothing got to him, not obnoxious duty assignments, not protocols, and not punishments, no matter how "Mickey Mouse" they appeared to be. He ostensibly followed orders, even if he only faked it. Tom was an irreverent Francis of Assisi, another of "God's Fools," smiling and joking his way through military life. Defiant, yet merry, he was unabashedly hysterical about the irony, absurdities, and the implausible reality that he was truly here. That was Tom, always a refreshing burst of fresh air.

Tom listed his religious preference as "The League of Spiritual Discovery," a pseudo-religious cult organized by Doctor Timothy Leary, the chief advocate of the powerful hallucinogen chemical Lysergic Acid Diethylamide (LSD). Tom could "blow your mind," as young people might say back in the day, and he did blow our minds with regularity. Like Rudy, the brass could not figure Tom out either.

Beyond all this, Tom was seriously anti-military and anti-war. We residents of the Bay of Pigs understood this perfectly. On the other hand, the brass and the NCOs had a very difficult time coming to grips with those whom they viewed as little more than slackers. Yet Tom was so much more than that—practicing mindfulness long before any of us learned of this teaching from the great Buddhist monk and friend of all Vietnam Veterans, Thich Nat Hahn.

Tom never feared the consequences of his actions. Picture this: Once, when he got fined for having his mustache too long, he responded by showing up at formation the next morning with half of it shaved off. The First Sergeant was crazy livid, red-faced and screaming. Tom, silent, a subtle half-smile under his newly customized facial hair, was immediately escorted to the stockade.

Tom was our court jester. If you were down about something all you had to do was spend some time with him and watch him work. He was a firm believer in the message of love advocated by so many in our generation, that we could make the world a better place, but only if the love started within each of us. Tom tried to show the way; we loved him for this and for who he was. Both Howie and Tom kept us laughing and happy, arming us with weapons much more potent than any we had mastered in the military.

Proud and erect, Jeff could demonstrate a bit of a sharp tongue, especially when confronting what many of us saw as the absurdities of military discipline and life. He was nobody's fool and was not about to be pushed around or controlled. An avid reader with keen insights and a quick wit, Jeff was a young man deeply affected by the countercultural promise of a more egalitarian society and the creation of a better world.

Jeff admitted to experiencing some adjustment problems in school and society. I suspect the knowledge he accumulated over the years made him intolerant of societal attempts to mold him into a mundane and cooperative factotum. Once Jeff told me he "conscientiously opposed" a lot of things, especially the Vietnam War which he considered the epitome of all things insane in American society.

Jeff wanted nothing to do with the war. As a civilian confronted with the uncertainty of being drafted, he sought the advice of a military recruiter. The thought of becoming a medic in a noncombatant role appeased him somewhat, and he discussed this possibility with the recruiter. Jeff was not told how he might be able to do this, and the recruiter did not agree to send him to Fort Sam Houston for medical training. Rather, Jeff was told he should sign up for the army and simply relay his wishes to the Company Commander during Basic Training. Encouraged, he trusted the advice and joined the army, sadly deceived like so many others. Jeff's enlistment helped the recruiter meet his monthly quota, but it left Jeff in a complicated situation that would challenge his conscience and change his life.

"AJ," another resident of the Bay of Pigs, frequently came in and out of our group. He was a quiet, thoughtful, cautious, and often detached guy. For example, he was uneasy about being photographed. I came to suspect he was worried about moles from military intelligence, perhaps even placed in the Bay of Pigs. I do not remember much about AJ's look or personality. But he was against the war and militarism, and the two of us later took a stand together in an attempt to change the military culture.

"Covington" was a guy with a very short fuse. As a civilian, he had been trained to work in the medical field, something akin to a medical technician. He seemed to feel at ease only when on duty at an infirmary. Covington was sharp tongued, easily provoked, and tended to see things negatively. The sun might be shining and the sky clear, but he was unaffected, as if perpetually hunkered down under his own dark and threatening cloud. He knew he was in the wrong place and was not about to be sent to Vietnam. As time went on, he had great difficulty putting up with anything he did not agree with. Like AJ, Covington was a bit on the outskirts of our clique, but we kept an eye on him and from time to time tried to calm him down.

I never saw the mysterious Hispanic troop we will call "Monte." From what I heard, he could be a bit of a handful, but I am not sure what that entailed. In any case, he also wanted nothing to do with the war in Vietnam and apparently was quite outspoken about it. Again, when I arrived in the Bay of Pigs, he was in the infirmary recovering from some ailment I cannot recall. Although he was absent from the barracks, we would shortly be affected by issues related to his situation.

———•———

And me? I was still a fledgling antiwar activist and far from a committed politico. I could be found somewhere in a universe of blossoming academic conjecture and abstract spiritual thinking. I also identified deeply with the youth culture, that is, our sense of community and the music and thoughts of social change. Unlike Tom, I was on the outskirts of hippiedom; and I would straddle the world of alternative choices for many years to come. Unlike Richard, I was no philosopher, not a healer like Rudy, nor an artist like Howie. Jeff and I shared a very important connection, although our demeanors were very different; that is, we both married young and soon both of our wives would be around Ft. Lewis providing us additional support and grounding the other guys did not have.

During my Catholic schooling, I internalized a message that challenged students to look for our "better angels," to step out of our "comfort zones," and to "walk the talk," especially when it came to following one's conscience. We were drilled in the differences between right and wrong and, although I often committed a lot of wrong, I had internalized the message and had great difficulty seeing anything right about the Vietnam War.

I came to the army with only two years of junior college, little more than a half-baked academic. Still, I knew enough, and I had read enough. Indeed, I learned so much during my twelve years in Catholic school that I had become truly disappointed with college. The course work, especially in the Liberal Arts, repeated most of the material we had gone over many times in grammar and high school. For the most part, I found college to be boring and considered it a waste of time.

I did have one remarkable learning experience in the class of a man who did not fit the stereotype I had of college professors. An American History instructor, this guy was a loose cannon; he violated current academic protocol in many ways including not wearing a tie, and much to our astonishment he brought his dog to class. He was a serious intellectual and was very difficult on students, including me. He challenged us with issues transcending the accepted narrative on any number of issues, such as the internment of Japanese American citizens during World

War II. Controversial and acerbic, he was livid about the war in Vietnam and saw us as compliant lemmings being used by the government. He continually challenged us to get off our butts and do something to oppose the war.

This professor's demeanor and rejection of school norms appealed to me, as did his provocative remarks on several topics. I liked and respected him, but it turns out I was in the minority. Many students could not stand him or his ideas; during class, they were rude to him in an attempt to get him to fly off the handle. For example, once he taught a seminar filled with students from three history classes. The student audience took to snapping their zippo lighters and clicking their pens to distract him and ultimately get him to explode. I was astounded by their behavior and it only made me listen even more closely to what this visionary had to offer. His critical approach, polemics, and challenges to the students impressed me. I learned things from him, ways to think critically, ways to reject the existing narrative, and ways to do something about the things in American society that upset us. These were valuable lessons that were beginning to surface and would soon be put into play.

Thirty-Second

—•—

Write On!

If you want to help other people
you have got to make up your mind
to write things some will condemn.

Rev. Thomas Merton, OCSO

Somehow, I got my hands on a typewriter and went to work on the application for discharge. The Bay of Pigs was empty most of the day, offering me much quiet time. The barracks did not have any desks, so I put the typewriter on the edge of my bunk, got on my knees, and typed away in a spontaneous, totally unconscious prayer for success.

Ten days to write! Unbelievable. This was my job, my "Temporary Duty Assignment." In the past, there were school and college deadlines to meet. There were always book reviews and papers to write for high school teachers and term papers for college professors. In both cases, this work was sandwiched around classes, after-school and weekend jobs, and trying to juggle a social life. But this time, I had ten whole days with few conflicting obligations. Never before did I have so much time to think and write.

My daily task was limited to hitting the mess hall for meals; otherwise for those ten days, time was mine. In my limited experience, I could only compare responding to the conscientious objector (C.O.) application to writing a school term paper; the most important one I would ever write. I literally rolled up my fatigue sleeves and got to it; the workaholism, which I did not then realize I had, kicked in and I began to type.

Sometimes I would get off my knees to walk around the barracks, as much to clear my head as to rethink my approach or review what I had drafted. It all felt natural, and I do not remember ever experiencing writer's block. At times, I would take a break from writing to find a phone and call potential references or contact various antiwar GI and civilian support groups. A few times I went to the base library to read or to match an idea with a source. But most of the day, I was in the dorm, thinking and typing, typing and thinking.

When I wrote at night, the guys all understood and gave me space. Sometimes though, I would simply hang out with them, comparing stories and picking their brains. But I let no one read or edit my stuff. This was mine. I was not looking for an editor or reviewer.

— • —

DoD 1300.6 contained three sections, each with several questions; a fourth section asked for a list of references. Reading my narrative some fifty years later, I see I glossed over some issues and took some liberties in addressing others. Sometimes the naïve young man I was would drift off-topic, providing information that went way beyond the subject at hand. Sometimes, I took things for granted and demonstrated a lack of specificity in places. At other times, formulations appeared that advanced dubious, youthful, false equivalents. Quite simply, at that time in my life, right was right and wrong was wrong, with few exceptions and no room for ambiguity. I reproduce the sections I wrote then below, changed or corrected only for clarity.

The applicant was asked to provide detail on himself/herself and others, religious training and belief, and specifics regarding participation in various organizations. In the first section, the focus was on demographic issues including the religious persuasion of parents as well as detail on the applicant's education and employment.

Applicants were also asked if they previously applied for conscientious objector status from the Selective Service System and any decision made by the board. Relatedly, the army still wanted to know if an applicant would perform alternative civilian service (for up to two years) if discharged with less than 180 days of military service.

In response to the two latter items, I told them I had indeed asked Selective Service to send Form 150; however, because my beliefs were not yet fully formulated then, I had refrained from sending it back, writing: "I was not completely convinced of or satisfied with my religious objections to war at that time."

Also, I already had 150 days of military service, with no idea how long the C.O. process would take. But in my case, no matter how many days of service I had—even more than 180—I agreed to voluntarily engage in the Selective Service's conscientious objector work program for the remainder of the two-year draft service requirement.

The all-important section on religious training and belief followed. This series of items constituted the meat of the matter. I found this part to be really tough and worked and reworked it for a couple of days. First, applicants were asked to describe the nature of their beliefs that formed the basis for their claim. For the most part I approached it this way, saying:

> As…a Roman Catholic, I know war in most cases is unnecessary, wrong, and unjust…. According to the Church today, a person can be both a good Christian and a soldier based on the individual conscience. All people owe a certain amount of allegiance to the civil authority that governs them, but there are many ways of expressing allegiance or patriotism.
>
> Religion, however, is of a higher order…. Government can never infringe on one's religious beliefs…. Christ wants us to love our neighbor as ourself. This is a grave and difficult duty…. I find there is…a duty to express my objection to war.

The next item wanted to know about the people, events, or training received that led the applicant to their beliefs about conscientious objection. I included the following material:

> Being born into a strict Catholic family and attending twelve years of parochial school…I referred to texts, histories, Bibles, etc. that have always been part of my religious training. I was the head of my local Catholic Youth Organization…we made it a point to help the young and

visit the sick of the town…I came in close contact with many priests as well as secular individuals dedicated to Christ's teachings…I realized the world was jarred occasionally by the violence of war…I have been drawn more to Christ's words in the New Testament in my own religious meditations.

Another item asked for contact information for an individual the applicant relied on for religious guidance, especially in matters related to the claim. Here, I pointed to the current pope, Pope Paul VI, writing, "All previous modern-day Popes had prevention of war among his primary aims." I also spoke to finding guidance from the Catholic Conference of Bishops in interpreting church teaching. By default, I admitted there was no one special acquaintance I relied on for guidance in this matter. Rather, I found proper guidance in sermons and readings and by looking within myself.

The next item asked for circumstances where the applicant believed in the use of force. I was still struggling mightily with the concept of nonviolent resistance. The notion was still relatively new to me and it seemed to rub up against both masculinity and Catholic tradition. I knew I was far from being a pacifist; clearly, I had been thoroughly trained to injure and kill. I already learned I could pull the trigger on a man and deep down knew something living inside me could do all the things they had trained me to do.

Intrinsically, I also knew violence was not something I wanted to unleash. To my young mind, it seemed if I were to reject the use of violence in war then I should also be able to cast it off when it came to using violence in general. This conundrum was another false equivalent I struggled with at the time. That said, I knew participating in the war in Vietnam was something I should not do, even if I was at a loss when it came to making a total commitment to nonviolence.

In my written response, I tried to interpret the question about using force to the singular decision of using it in a war. Then, drilling down to personal situations, I said,

> The use of force in protecting one's rights of life…or in the protection of an innocent person…under physical attack can be justified…and properly constitutes a right to use force for self-preservation if all else fails. However, one must remember the words of the papal encyclical, Pacem in Terris: "Violence has always achieved only destruction, not construction."

Projecting, I went on to say:

> The strongest, most powerful people in the world are those who can meet an adversary face-to-face and overcome the danger through the nonviolent use of force. This is the only use of force to which I can conscientiously subscribe.

—•—

The next section wanted a description of the applicant's actions and behavior demonstrating the depth of conviction that gave rise to the conscientious objector claim.

This item was also extremely difficult for me to answer. I had not been raised in one of the traditionally recognized peace churches such as the Mennonites or the Quakers; therefore, I ran into few adults who advocated world peace. Except for union men who used shop stewards to solve problems and work stoppages to make changes, I had rarely been exposed to people who worked for nonviolent social change. For some unknown reason, my periodic youthful involvement and support of the civil rights movement did not seem applicable. Nor did my respect for the Rev. Martin Luther King, Jr., who dramatically demonstrated how to work for change by using nonviolent means. At this point, I did not understand seeking justice *was* working for peace. Even the occasional letters I sent to Congress on a variety of issues, including the war in Vietnam, did not seem to address the query. Wasn't this just proper behavior for Americans wanting to peacefully petition their government for change?

However, I did find it easy to link my personal actions and behaviors to religious training and practice. Innocently, I assumed this involvement would speak for itself. Naïvely, I imagined it would be easy to understand how this led me down the path to conscientious objection. Therefore, instead of discussing my previous civilian experiences, I focused on my current situation, especially what I had learned in infantry training and the interactions I had with troops who were having doubts or just wanted to talk about the war. I penned this:

> One must obey Christ's order, each in his or her own way. I find the best method is…to present Christian ideals through individual actions. Since my entry into the service, my views on war and killing have crystallized to the point where I must express them openly. I now assume the duty of a Christian conscientious objector. This essay, I believe, stands as the greatest proof of my conviction.
>
> I have found little chance of expressing beliefs on any grand scale while in the military, except of course to my

peers. However, I have assumed responsibility and done what I am required, according to my religion.

Before my entry into the military, I was considered … a good Catholic. I attended Mass, received the sacraments, etc. These things are important. However, the army has shown me I was paying more attention to the ritual than to human beings. Now I see it is my duty to refuse to kill people; now I see it is imperative I leave the military and help my country through peaceful means; now I see I must return to civilian life and teach the truths I have discovered.

— • —

The final item in this section sought specifics on written or public expression made relevant to the C.O. claim. In part, I responded this way:

I expound my views on this subject to anyone who wants to listen. There is no real opportunity to express myself publicly while in the army, however I have asserted my beliefs time and again to those with whom I came in contact. The men with whom I took advanced infantry training … know that my religious convictions offer no justification for my being in the service.

These views … did not gain life and strength until after I entered the service. Except for letters to home and friends, this is the only written record of my religious objection to war. It … will remain in my file whether the government … ignores my claim or accepts it …. In any case I am proud to be a conscientious objector.

The last section wanted to know about participation in various organizations. The first four items listed here were fairly straightforward. One wanted to know if I had ever been a member of a military organization prior to being drafted. The second wanted to know if I was a member of a religious organization including the name and location of my parish and the name and address of the pastor. Here, I had to admit I was only marginally involved in the parish but had been actively engaged in my parish's Catholic Youth Organization. I did not mention the Congress of Racial Equality; I foolishly downplayed this formative experience and I could not remember if I ever joined the organization.

The next item asked about the creed or official statements of the Church and required a more detailed response. Here are some excerpts from my reply, ones that might have resonance today in Ukraine and Russia:

The Church recognizes the duty of love, reverence, and obedience every person owes to the state; however, it also teaches that "my country right or wrong" is an immoral model to which a Christian cannot possibly subscribe. War, according to St. Thomas Aquinas, shall be used as a last resort, with the "good outweighing the evil," and it must be waged to right a wrong "not simply to maintain national prestige or enlarge territory." Aquinas wrote, "Those who intend actively to take part in a war that has already broken out must first be morally certain of its justness."

On preventive war, Pope Pius XII said, "A nation cannot resort to force simply because it suspects...an enemy attack. There must be an actual attack or clear factual evidence of its imminence." The pope declared that a defensive war "to preserve national security and freedom is morally admissible." But he called the war of aggression "an offense and outrage against the majesty of God."

The Second Vatican Council's Constitution urged support for national leaders who work to stop wars. The national conference of bishops…urged personal freedom "based on individual conscience and God alone." They also voted…in favor of conscientious objection. The Council also suggested "that laws make human provision for those who for reasons of conscientious objection refused to bear arms provided however that they agreed to serve the human community in some other way."

The Church has always held that in the case of an unjust war a Catholic would be bound in duty to refuse to take part in it, i.e., he or she would have to be a conscientious objector.

Christianity requires all people to search their consciences and establish their beliefs, otherwise they are neither patriotic nor religious.

———•———

Finally, I listed four references who had agreed to send correspondence regarding the sincerity of my beliefs. The first was my friend and mentor, the Rev. Louis A. Leyh, from my childhood parish. I included Dennis, the man I debated in Advanced Infantry Training. Also, I listed two civilian friends—one a lifelong buddy and a member of our parish, the other a brilliant, slightly older fellow who became a friend and an intellectual touchstone during my CYO days.

About mid-week I put the early drafts aside to attend the required meetings with the psychiatrist and a chaplain to whom I had been assigned.

That, as some might say, "was a party!"

Thirty-Third

•

Twists of Fate

The journey never happens alone.

Rev. Richard Rohr, OFM

I was looking forward to my interview with the chaplain. I kept thinking of the marvelous interactions I had during my Catholic Youth Organization (CYO) days under the tutelage of my mentor, the Rev. Louis A. Leyh. The priests I knew were gracious, giving, approachable, and for the most part happy. Priests were important people in my life; they were wise, helpful, and forgiving. The chaplains' assistant who scheduled the meeting did not offer me a choice of Catholic chaplains; but I had no reason to believe the holy man I was slated to encounter would be much different than those priests I had experienced in civilian life.

What I did not know was that "Father K" was the Deputy Post Chaplain and a Lieutenant Colonel. In the U.S. Army, that meant he held a rank one step below Colonel and two ranks from Brigadier General. This priest was an important guy.

To achieve the rank of Lieutenant Colonel, a soldier had to be a serious lifer; I guessed back then he had to have more than twenty years of military service. That was apparent as soon as I was summoned to enter Fr. K's office. He was much older than any officer I ever met. He stood ramrod straight and snapped an impressive salute, his brilliant silver oak leaf insignia flashed like a warning sign from his lapel. My brain went on immediate alert, encouraging me to be cool and careful. I told myself, *Hey, this man's a priest. He probably brought a great deal of comfort to many troops over his long tenure in the military.*

After exchanging salutes, the chaplain rather brusquely told me to sit down on the opposite side of his big, immaculate desk, asking, "Why are you here?" He became more hostile from there. I was immediately put on the defensive, even as I tried to honor the cloth and respect his rank.

Fr. K kept peppering me with rapid fire questions that had absolutely nothing to do with war or war resistance. Instead, he focused on being dismissive and seemed fixated on the use of force in personal situations. For example, he asked "What would you do if you were being robbed?" and "What would you do if you saw someone try to rape a family member?" I had rarely been put back on my heels like this, and certainly not by a member of the clergy. We spent very little time discussing the ways in which the teachings of the Church coincided with my beliefs on conscientious objection.

———•———

As things got testy, I became more frustrated and intimidated. At that point in my life, I did not have enough experience to know how to turn a hostile confrontation like this toward dialog.

I tried not to say anything harsh, rash, or judgmental, but I did begin to verbally stand up to him. Unbelievably, he appeared to want me to get angry or say or do something stupid. I didn't fall into that trap, but I did parry his verbal attacks. I am quite sure my words and body language indicated I was no longer being deferential.

Fr. K could not believe there was a religious basis to my claim and suggested all conscientious objectors were slackers trying to put something over on the military. Being dismissive, he said something like "now and again your kind comes here looking for discharges..." and told me he considered my beliefs to be—and I am absolutely quoting him here—"crap."

During our final exchange, he wanted to know which "subversive organizations" I joined. When I angrily responded, "just the Catholic Church," he lost it. He grabbed my arm, pushed me, and in no uncertain terms ordered me to "Get out!" We did not even exchange the required parting salutes. I just turned and stormed out.

Think about this for a minute. I had just literally been thrown out of a chaplain's office! Soldier or not, this man was a Catholic priest, but he offered no guidance and certainly was not sympathetic or interested in my beliefs. I walked away from there realizing he had not given me a fair hearing but had been focused on trying to trip me up.

I tried to calm down on my way back to the barracks. I knew I could not continue to obsess about this. I had to concentrate, retype and finalize the draft of my application for conscientious objector status before handing it in. I kept telling myself I just met a hard-core soldier, a Lieutenant Colonel of all things, a soldier first and foremost who perhaps on Sundays transformed himself into a soldier of Christ. Well, I guessed to myself, *Michael the Archangel, the patron saint of warfare, would be proud of him.*

Still, I tried not to be judgmental. After all, these clerics had made conscious decisions to live as soldiers and as ministers at the same time. There is no question the troops needed them to help with personal and familial issues, to offer comfort, and to share sacred stories. I was not ready to give up on them yet; even if the negative experience with Fr. K cut deep and was hard to forgive.

A few days later his three-sentence interview statement arrived. It simply said, "The basis for his objection is not a religious interpretation of the Catholic faith."

———•———

The next day I went for the psychiatric evaluation. The captain conducting the interview was indeed a psychiatrist. Somewhat bemused, but focused and introspective, he asked some benign pro forma questions and we bounced around several ideas. It was a relatively short meeting and within a couple of days I received a copy of his statement. The brief two paragraph response said I was "relevant, coherent, and the beliefs or reasons for claiming conscientious objection do not appear to be influenced in any way by significant mental aberration." His conclusion was simply that I did not suffer from any mental disease or derangement.

There was no question, however, that some of the other officers I encountered did not feel the same way.

For the next couple days, I put the final touches on my conscientious objector application. I made some changes, adding material on my experience with Father K. and with other chaplains I had observed throughout my training. I finalized the application and handed it in. I also sent a copy of Fr. K's short summary of our meeting to Chas Talbot and the Catholic Peace Fellowship, hoping they could assist in countering his views.

The next day I went to speak with the duty officer, hoping he would permanently assign me to work one of the mess halls while we awaited a decision on my conscientious objector claim. That said, I really suspected he would send me to some obnoxious outdoor assignment like mucking latrines or walking around picking up cigarette butts.

Staff-Sergeant "Nails" was the unit's duty officer, the manager of the orderly room. Nails was a starched and polished NCO who was in it for the long haul. He was a bit short but held his head high, and like so many other NCOs, he took his job very seriously. He was detail-oriented, efficient, deferential to officers while doing what had to be done to process the paperwork and complete never-ending administrative chores.

He asked me, "What are your skills?" I said, "Well, I'm a pretty good typist," and before I could talk about restaurant work, he stopped me in my tracks saying, "Wait, wait, you can type, not finger pick?" I said, "Sure, at least 50 words per minute." His expression changed, his eyes widened, he smiled broadly and in a gleeful, expletive-laden moment of pure gratitude proclaimed, "Hot Damn, I got one! Outstanding! You start right now."

It seemed like the handful of clerks in the orderly room respected him, so I was tempted to agree. Given his reaction, I suspected my chances of being assigned to the mess hall would be ignored and, considering other possible details, the idea of working inside during the winter appealed to me. But I did have one issue we needed to discuss. I said, "Okay Sarge, but you need to know I put in for two-week leave that overlaps Christmas. That means I will only be here for a short time and won't return until shortly after New Year's Day. I know you will have to sign off on my request, so I hope this will not be a problem."

I could tell Nails was still giddy about the whole thing. We discussed the dates and he told me not to worry about it. He assured me only a skeleton crew would be on the base during the holidays. During this time the office slowed down because fewer troops on the base meant less work for him. Pulling rank, he told me to make sure I did not request any additional leave time and come back to work when I said I would. In the meantime, he would get me trained, have me work with a couple of other clerks, and assign me some tasks. I was immediately given a desk and some handwritten documents to type.

Sergeant Nails was happy, I was relieved; neither one of us truly understood what we were about to get ourselves into.

I worked in the orderly room for the next several days learning about its mission and the tasks that needed to be addressed. Once my leave was approved, I approached Nails with another request. I told him I would like to return with my wife and live off the base until my case was adjudicated. He said he would take it up with the Company Commander. Given my situation, I did not believe this request was going to be honored, but I made preparations for the drive back just in case. To my great surprise, the request was approved, and I would be allowed to live off base.

The plan was to leave Jersey the day after Christmas, arriving in Washington State several days later. This would allow for a couple days to rent a place before having to report to the orderly room.

With the leave approved, I phoned the Sea-Tac airport to reserve a seat for a flight back to New Jersey. The customer representative told me to come to the airport in uniform with a military ID and I would be given a substantial military discount. She told me to simply check in on the day of the flight, pay for and pick-up my reserved ticket.

At the time, there were a lot of rumors floating around about GIs being confronted by civilians upset with the war. From what little I knew it seemed pretty benign and as far as I was concerned, very encouraging. It seemed like antiwar folks were at the airport handing out fliers while trying to engage the troops whenever and wherever they could. Frankly, I thought this would be interesting and, if it happened to me, could be a moment of solidarity. The brass, however, took this development seriously, insisting there were many occasions when troops got into verbal or physical confrontations with antiwar activists. Before the holidays, we were issued strong directives on how to dress and behave in public areas.

I had not heard any stories from other grunts about these altercations, but some guys I ran into were concerned. In their frustration, some civilians did not fully understand that GIs did not start this war and many of us opposed it. On the other hand,

I ran into a fair number of troops who supported the war and a greater number who seemed to have a very, very, short fuse about it. If any of these stories were true, I thought, I could see how easily such situations might get out of hand. In any case, I wanted to see what was really going on and whether or not antiwar activists were trying to engage or antagonize military guys.

———•———

I was a pretty strack-looking troop when I got to the airport. I wore nicely pressed Dress Greens, with shined brass and polished shoes. Uncomfortably overdressed yes, but it was worth it. I had just enough money to cover the discounted military ticket with only a few dollars left in my wallet. Sea-Tac airport in Seattle was crowded with holiday travelers. There was a lot of hustle and bustle, but absolutely no one was engaged in any type of antiwar activity. Some military guys scurried about, but I did not detect any incidents.

In those days one could not check-in or pay for a ticket electronically. You had to do that at the airline counter. The long queue at the check-in counter reminded me of the lines often found outside the mess hall and the old military adage, "Hurry up and wait." When it was finally my turn, I gave the clerk the information on my reservation. She thumbed through some papers and told me there had been a mistake. The airline did not offer military rates during the holiday season. I was forty dollars short. This was devastating. There were no credit cards back then and, of course, no ATMs, not that I would have a checking account, no less one with forty dollars deposited. I confronted her repeating what I had been told when I ordered the ticket, but all she could do was apologize. When I demanded a resolution, she offered to hold the ticket while I visited Travelers Aid and the airport's USO to seek help.

I was grasping at straws, but I had to believe something could be arranged. Both of these places provided many services, but I soon discovered neither one would advance cash to stranded passengers. I called home to see if it was possible to wire some money, but for some reason this did not work out. The only thing I could do was return to the counter and plead my case with a supervisor, hoping the airline would bill me, especially if I agreed to pay the money immediately upon landing. Back in line, I finally made it to the same clerk who "helped" me before.

I related my tale of woe and how neither organization would lend the money. The clerk and her supervisor were sympathetic but firm. The plane was full. It was about to board. There were people on standby. Nothing could be done. I had to give up the ticket. Suddenly, as if by wizardry, a hand containing two twenty-dollar bills appeared over my right shoulder. The guy behind me had heard the story, empathized completely, and agreed to lend me the money.

The army brass had been right. I had just been confronted by a civilian.

Thank God this guy already had a seat. Trying not to get too emotional, I assured him I would pay him back when we got to Jersey, thanked him profusely, and headed off to the gate. I'll tell you what, that old curmudgeon Andrew Jackson never looked so good.

I called home saying everything worked out and made sure money would be available to repay this Good Samaritan. Many have suggested that "Saints do walk this Earth." That day I met one.

Thirty-Fourth

—•—

"You Always Hurt the One You Love"

"The one you shouldn't hurt at all."

Allan Roberts and Doris Fisher

Our telephone conversation went very much like this.
"Hi, Mom, it's Jerry."
A brief exchange of small talk.
"Listen Mom. I want to tell you we made it to Washington State and rented a little cabin just a short drive to the base."
Words of surprise and questions about moving off the base.
"We immediately found a place and moved right in. My landlord is a short, Elmer Fudd looking guy, with a small home-stead and a horse named Pickles. He was more than happy to rent one of his three small cabins to GIs from Fort Lewis. The cabins were in a wood-covered area a bit off the beaten path. It is really close to a large lake with a dock for pontoon planes that fly in for water landings. It's pretty cool.

"From now on, I won't be living with my friends in the barracks, but otherwise it was easy to move out of the dormitory. Plus, the army will grant a small monthly housing allowance to supplement my meager monthly pay.

"But that is not really why I called. I made some decisions you and Dad need to know about. First of all, do you remember I was talking to you about being classified as a conscientious objector by the draft board? Well, as you know I did not feel comfortable doing that, so I did not apply. But now that I have been trained in so many things, I see stuff much more clearly. I know what it's all about. I know this is something I should not do. I decided I cannot participate in this war. So, I filed for conscientious objector status and will be on temporary hold at Fort Lewis until the case is adjudicated."

A worried and questioning reaction.

"Yeah, it is a normal procedure. It's late in the game I know, but this is within the military's administrative code and it is perfectly legal for me to do this. I am being helped by the Catholic Peace Fellowship and by an attorney in Seattle, so yeah, I am playing by all the rules."

A sad and anxious sigh.

"Here's the thing. This process could take the army a little bit of time to figure out. The paperwork has already been sent to Washington, DC, for review. You should know there is a chance it will not be approved, but I would get an appeal process asking them to reconsider. If the claim is approved, I will be honorably discharged and coming back home. However, you need to know there is a chance the claim will not be accepted and I will face a choice. The choice is either to ship to Vietnam or to be imprisoned at a Federal prison in Kansas."

A plaintive, "Oh…." Deep concern and questions about the procedure.

"Well, you get court-martialed, the military equivalent of going to court. But the case is heard by officers, not a judge, and on extremely narrow grounds. The question becomes did I refuse orders or not. It may have little to do with my beliefs or the merits of the war.

"It's not easy to win at a court-martial, so the chances are they will rule against me and, if I continue to refuse to ship, I could end up dishonorably discharged and spend anywhere from one to three years imprisoned at Fort Leavenworth. Mom, you know going to jail goes against everything I've been taught. But, this whole court-martial thing is about the law versus your conscience. I feel good with it. It took a long time to get to this place, but I believe this is what needs to be done to stand up for what I believe and to help end the war.

"So, I need you not to worry, Mom. From watching the news, you know all over the country there are a lot of us who feel this way. Again, I guess I should have taken action on this much earlier, but I really thought through dialogue and by talking with people on the draft board and in the army, they would under-stand I was in the wrong place and should be discharged; but this was not meant to be. So, I feel formally registering my objec-tion is the correct way to go. Anyway, I will keep you informed and will let you know how things shake out. Tell Dad and say some prayers, and I will do the rest. Whatever that is; whatever that turns out to be."

There was another deep sigh and a long pause. Then, in a voice quivering in fear, worry, and love, this gentle, Catholic working-class elder, a witness to two world wars and the Depression replied with words that cut deep and still move me all these decades later: "Oh Jerry, you'll never get a job."

Thirty-Fifth

——●——

Rising Up

The greatest challenge of the day is
how to bring about a revolution of the heart,
a revolution which has to start with each one of us.

Dorothy Day

The Shelter Half Coffeehouse was a project of Seattle's GI-Civilian Alliance for Peace (GI-CAP). The storefront took its name from a moniker applied to half a military tent. A shelter half could be used by one guy or joined with another half to create shelter for two men. The coffeehouse was a local hub for GIs, veterans, and local peace activists. This was the antiwar alternative to traditional USOs; a relaxing facility for GIs to meet, unwind, and listen to music. Folks could grab light snacks, gather together for small group rap sessions, or attend various presentations from activists involved in the peace movement.

The Shelter Half was staffed by both civilians and antiwar veterans. In addition to running the storefront, they organized demonstrations and provided GIs with brochures and leaflets to hand out to others. Most importantly, typewriters and mimeograph machines were available for use by active-duty troops. In addition, the staff worked with soldiers to produce *Counterpoint*, an underground antiwar newspaper. GIs would grab leaflets or newspapers and clandestinely distribute them around the base by placing them in latrines, bus stations, and places where troops congregated.

The Coffeehouse was under constant surveillance, and everyone knew it. Fearing a set-up, a very large sign at the front entrance announced alcohol and drugs were strictly prohibited. The place was adorned with psychedelic posters and counter-culture slogans protesting the war and announcing various antiwar events being held around the country.

—•—

Our Bay of Pigs contingent joined other active-duty GIs and Vietnam veterans who showed up periodically at The Shelter Half to chill out and talk about opposition to the war. At one meeting, a representative of the American Civil Liberties Union talked about forming an ACLU chapter at Fort Lewis. One night, a petition was circulated for folks wishing to join the base chapter. This appealed to AJ and me, and we both signed the sheet.

It was not illegal (or even all that radical) to join organizations like the ACLU, and the two of us did not suspect repercussions for taking this action; although I could not imagine the brass would allow an organization on base working to protect the civil liberties of the troops under their command. Still, promoting a base chapter was another way for grunts like us to align with civilians and express our deep dissatisfaction with arbitrary actions meant to keep us quiet and under control.

Staff at the Shelter Half were also organizing on behalf of the first three GIs convicted of mutiny for being part of the so-called "Presidio 27" in California. In October 1968, twenty-seven prisoners at the Presidio stockade in San Francisco sat down and sang the song "We Shall Overcome" to protest the recent killing of another prisoner and conditions at the stockade. They presented a list of grievances seeking improved prison conditions and expressing opposition to the Vietnam War. The twenty-seven guys were all arrested after ignoring orders to disperse. The first three men tried were each convicted of mutiny and sentenced to 14-16 years of hard labor for participating in this nonviolent protest.

Staff of the Shelter Half provided preprinted support letters to be signed and sent to the Commanding General of the 6th U.S. Army. The letters asked the General to recognize the legitimacy of the prisoner's complaints, reverse the court's decision, and release the men. We soldiers were encouraged to grab some, hand them out at Fort Lewis, get signatures, and send them to the Presidio. I collected some signatures and mailed them off.

Years later, I was able to confirm we were all under observation. It turns out an agent from Military Intelligence was at the Shelter Half the night AJ and I signed to establish the Fort Lewis Chapter of the ACLU. This agent provided the list of all signatories to the base commanders. The Deputy Chief of Staff of Intelligence for the U.S. Army also notified the Department of Defense that I had forwarded letters to the Presidio protesting the mutiny trials. In both cases, documents by or about me were filed as exhibits.

Unknown to me, I was becoming famous, or perhaps infamous, in my little corner of the military, not something I sought, but not something I ran away from either.

———•———

Over the next several months, our fellowship of resisters periodically hung out at the Shelter Half. It was comfortable there, we learned a lot, and we were surrounded with like spirits all seeking to end the war. We were among the now rapidly growing number of GIs beginning to resist the war throughout the nation. In the coffeehouse, guys were sitting around, talking about the war, discussing politics, and planning further resistance. Getting together with the informal groups that gathered to do this was intensely rewarding to me and my buddies, especially the interaction we had with returned Vietnam combat veterans.

The act of simply getting together to express grievances about our treatment and the legitimacy of the war was grounds enough for the brass to worry. Besides their keeping a watchful eye on the place, we knew they were having ongoing discussions about making the Shelter Half off limits for all military personnel. The base commanders considered the Shelter Half a downright dangerous place, one providing a safe space for soldiers to freely engage with others of their own age who were all in the same situation. The guys were spreading dissension simply by getting together, talking, and taking action against the war. The way we saw it, one, this was America, two, the war was wrong, and three, as Americans we had a duty to speak our minds.

Several Bay of Pigs resisters headed to Seattle on February 16, 1969, to join other active military personnel in the announced GI-Civilian March for Peace in Seattle. Sources differ on attendance, but somewhere between 1,000 and 4,000 people attended this nonviolent demonstration. Most were civilians, but they were led by a large contingent of Vietnam veterans and active-duty GIs. You could recognize the vets from the ragtag collection of fatigues, camo gear, threadbare jungle boots, and field jackets that set them apart from the others. Some of them had peace signs or antiwar messages scribbled on the backs of their shirts or fatigues. Active-duty troops like me were not permitted to be in uniform when participating in political actions, but nevertheless our identities were apparent as many of us wore our black combat boots and all of us marched in the GI contingent.

This march was the most wonderful thing that had happened to me since I was drafted. We found ourselves surrounded by people of like mind, all exercising their right to gather peacefully and petition our government for change. These were folks of all ages and walks of life—marching, chanting and carrying American flags, banners, and signs—all demanding an end to the senseless, continued killing of Americans and Southeast Asians. Again, like Simon and Garfunkel, I felt like we'd, "All come to look for America". On this day, I knew I found it.

—•—

By 1969, dramatic, newsworthy examples of outright opposition to the war inside the military grew, as did AWOLs, desertions, court-martials, and imprisonments. However, everyday expressions of discontent were much less known. Few of these made the headlines, but in many and varied ways these were statements that affected military culture and, I firmly believe, helped end the draft and ultimately ended the war.

For example, as in-service resisters, we expected we would have to confront actual or low-level harassment in addition to outright tests of our sincerity. This happened periodically. Confrontations could include asking us to attend weapons training or to otherwise handle weaponry. Then again, there were seemingly inadvertent directives issued to conscientious objectors that violated existing protocols. This occurred when members of the Cadre were not aware of official procedures governing the treatment of conscientious objectors.

Once, while on the grounds outside the Bay of Pigs, a couple of us were approached by two of our E-5 sergeants. These were a couple of middle-aged, mild-mannered guys who were in the army for the long-term. Like so many of their colleagues, these noncommissioned officers made up the backbone of the entire army system, keeping the wheels of everyday military life churning. This was simply their job. It was easy to imagine each night after a day's work both these guys headed home to their families.

These men were used to giving and taking orders. They did what they were told and did not expect any trouble from underlings—especially from very young troops who often clearly mystified them. This was one of those times. One of the sergeants said, "I need you two to head over to the weapons room, pick up a couple of .38s and head over to the infirmary. We need you to guard Monte, one of your buddies."

Now *this* was interesting. On one hand, neither of us ever met the mysterious Monte or knew why he was in the infirmary. It would have been great to finally meet him and hear his story. On the other hand, given our status as conscientious objectors, we were not required to handle or use weapons.

We were not sure if this request was a test of our resolve, some low-level type of harassment, or just a terrible oversight on the part of these two guys. In any case, I watched one guy's jaw drop when we mentioned the regulation and advised him to check with the Company Commander for verification. These sergeants could not believe a couple of lowly privates would dare stand up to them and ignore a directive.

In the meantime, hoping to appease them, we offered to guard Monte without carrying weapons. Incredulous, one of the sergeants blurted out, "But what if he tries to escape!?" We simply told him not to worry about it, this guy should not be much of a problem, and we would stop him if he tried to leave the hospital.

On the plus side, we never heard from these noncoms again; conversely, I soon discovered we had not thought this whole thing out. Something was obviously going on over at the infirmary; we just did not grasp the whole picture or stop to consider just why our missing brother needed to be guarded. Instead, we told the story to the others at the Bay of Pigs as if it was one of those awkward moments of comic relief so frequently portrayed in a Shakespearean drama. This was a very bad mistake. A couple days later, we heard that Monte, the absent Hispanic resister few of us ever met, had left the hospital. But he did not go AWOL or desert, he was whisked away and sent to Vietnam. It was Monte who needed us to guard him, not the army.

No one seemed to know exactly what happened. The rumor was Monte had been placed under guard and transferred to the Overseas Replacement Center against his will. Had his C.O. application ever been adjudicated? Was it denied and then was he immediately ordered to ship? Was he really considered a threat to desert? Did these two E-5s actually expect the two of us to not only guard Monte but to actually help them pull off his transfer to Vietnam? We could not get any straight answers; all our unit's NCOs pleaded complete ignorance.

Guys at the Bay of Pigs were pretty upset about this. We concluded that some members of the brass bypassed regulations and took matters into their own hands, in this case by forcing the young man onto a plane against his will, while challenging the depth of our own sincerity as Vietnam war resisters. We never got a straight answer and thus we always assumed Monte had been railroaded. The bottom line was we never heard another word about or from Monte, and mysteriously the number of conscientious objectors at our site had abruptly decreased by one.

———•———

Another time, we had three guys in our unit who refused to attend training, in this case a Chemical and Biological Warfare exercise. Because the class centered around tear gas and gas mask training, the brass did not think it qualified under the protocol protecting conscientious objectors from handling or using weaponry. Conversely, the resisters thought this certainly *was* weapons training and considered it most likely related to civilian crowd control. The idea of handling weapons and learning to apply them for use against American citizens just did not sit well with these three men. Indeed, it did not sit well with most guys with whom I trained and worked.

The Judge Advocate General decided these three conscientious objectors should suffer a lower-level court martial known as a "Special Court." A conviction here could lead to fines and/

or imprisonment. All three were court martialed; one was sent to the stockade for a couple months. The other two received various sentences that included reductions in rank and forfeiture of some pay for a few months.

——•——

Some residents of the Bay of Pigs were in and out of the stockade for any number of petty offenses (like hitch-hiking). At some points, we came into contact with others from our Holding Company who were also in the stockade.

When our guys returned from the stockade, they reported on conditions and coping mechanisms useful during confinement. While there, they discovered most of the incarcerated were angry about being in the army and wanted out. We conscientious objectors saw this as an opportunity to convince the disaffected to take the next step and not cooperate with war making. Several soldiers outside the Bay of Pigs were intrigued by this position and some of them met with of us on base or at the Shelter Half when they were released from the stockade.

Besides outright resistance to command and control, all sorts of low-level transgressions seemed to occur as young draftees and recruits took matters into their own hands. For example, one day while I was typing in the Orderly Room, a general came stomping through. It happened so fast nobody yelled, "Attention!" But fairly quickly, everybody popped up and most offered halfhearted salutes as the overweight, notoriously drunk senior officer barged through one door and quickly disappeared through another.

I just kept typing. The ever proper, detailed oriented, and now completely frustrated Sergeant Nails approached me, with shocked disbelief and deep trepidation overshadowing his suppressed anger.

Nails: "You didn't stand up!"

Me: "I was busy."

Nails: "But … but … that was a general!"

Me: "He was half in the bag. I don't think he noticed."

Poor Sergeant Nails just stood there for a few seconds looking down on me. Then shaking his head in total confusion and mumbling under his breath, he returned to the safety of his desk.

———•———

We witnessed another demonstration of personal intolerance when our buddy Covington begrudgingly headed off for duty at a new medical facility. Upon arrival, he was told he was not needed there and should report to another unit in the same complex. Our resident Bay of Pigs hothead decided he had been pushed around one too many times. In his mind, he had tried to cooperate but was always being forced to compromise. Like our mate Rudy, as something of a medical professional Covington too just wanted to make people better; but he blamed all officers and Cadre for making things worse, especially for him.

That day he disappeared somewhere on the short walk between those two facilities. He never returned to the Bay of Pigs. About a month later we got a postcard from Canada. He was living as an expatriate approximately 200 miles away. We never heard from him again. Suddenly, we were down another resister.

We never lost our friend Tom completely, but in the succeeding months after Covington's departure, Tom was in and out of our lives. His mischief and free spirit led to a few administrative punishments, including the occasional foray to the stockade. You often hear people who have gone to prison say they never felt freer. Tom was one of those guys. He was free when he walked around Fort Lewis and was still the same guy when doing time in the base stockade.

Rudy's application for conscientious objector status had been denied shortly before I arrived at the Bay of Pigs. He was deemed a "selective objector" to a particular war, but, selective opposition to war was not allowed under military regulations. On the day before I submitted my request for discharge, Rudy refused to abide with orders to report to the Overseas Replacement Center for shipment to Vietnam. He was to be given a general court martial. Thankfully, he was not sent to the stockade to await trial. Instead, he was allowed to perform duties in the Garrison Company until he was court martialed.

His trial was held at the end of February. At a General Court, the defendant is tried by a panel of nine officers; no enlisted men, draftees, or noncommissioned officers sat in judgment. Sergeant Nails gave me permission to attend Rudy's trial, and as I recall a few of the others were also able to come to offer support and solidarity.

As expected, the case was adjudicated on extremely narrow grounds. That is, on the simple question of whether the accused was guilty of refusing a direct order. The legitimacy or morality of the war and the defendant's feelings about it were considered basically irrelevant. The legality and morality of the Vietnam War was as far away from being introduced as Exhibit A as Southeast Asia was from the borders of the United States.

Rudy's defense counsel was an officer from the Judge Advocate General's office. I believe a civilian attorney could also have been present or chosen to represent him, but Rudy decided to work within the military system. Honest and straightforward as ever, Rudy had pleaded guilty to willfully disobeying an order to ship to Vietnam during a pre-trial conference. The only issue to be determined was whether he would be confined for any length of time at Fort Leavenworth prison in Kansas.

The prosecuting law officer did everything in his power to keep a discussion of the war out of the proceedings. The defense attorney attempted to portray Rudy as the conscientious, extremely cooperative troop he actually was. The attorney tried to show Rudy was not anti-military but rather totally against any sort of participation in the Vietnam War.

The defense called one of the officers in our unit who attested to Rudy's military bearing, cooperation, and initiative. When asked, this officer replied, "I do not feel a period of confinement would be serving justice in this case."

Our First Sergeant, who could not attend the proceedings, echoed this sentiment in a statement he provided in Rudy's defense. He called Rudy "a man of outstanding character" and said, "I would rather see him discharged for the good of the service…because of his strong personal conviction."

Much to my pleasure and surprise, Sergeant Nails also testified for the defense. Among other accolades, he called Rudy, "one of the most reliable individuals I've ever had work for me." When asked if conscientious objectors should be jailed for disobeying an order, Nails replied, "That would depend on his other actions, character, criminal intent…whether or not he had a belligerent attitude…." (Nails also inadvertently confirmed our suspicions we had all been grouped together at the Bay of Pigs by admitting our First Sergeant wanted all conscientious objectors placed in one unit, "Right there, under his thumb.")

Rudy gave succinct, heartfelt, and brilliant responses to questions posed by the defense and prosecuting attorneys. After both sides presented their closing arguments, the hearing officer issued instructions to the jury, who then adjourned to deliberate.

Those of us who came to support Rudy hung around for the sentence. The tension was thick and ominous, even as we hoped for the best. We were a bundle of nerves, but all of us were in it for the long haul. One of the guys suggested the longer the officers deliberated, the better it was for Rudy. Perhaps he would be fined and released with a Bad Conduct Discharge. Those hopes were shattered when the panel returned a mere twenty-seven minutes later with their sentence: confinement at hard labor for two years, forfeiture of all pay and allowances, and a dishonorable discharge.

After sentencing, and true to form, Rudy maintained his military bearing, orchestrated a perfect salute, pirouetted into a smooth about-face, and proudly stepped off to meet his future. I believe some applauded as he marched by. I wanted to sing a protest song, but at the last second thought better of it, fearing Rudy might be blamed for the outburst.

Rudy was now the third man permanently gone from the Bay of Pigs contingent. He was an inspiration and guiding light for all of us. We learned a lot from his character, behavior, and witness. Especially that day, when he showed us how to stick to our beliefs and carry ourselves with dignity and pride as we confronted our adversities.

— • —

It had been a wild, educational, and productive first few months of 1969. I felt motivated, strengthened, and inspired by all the good antiwar work that seemed to be going on. I also felt I was doing some good in the orderly room by helping guys with everyday military problems and clandestinely advising those who were having qualms about the war.

It should be stressed I was not alone when it came to counseling guys who were having serious problems about the war. Several guys at the Bay of Pigs met with troops at the holding company, in our barracks, at the PX, and in the stockade. To our great surprise, we discovered that, in addition to Sergeant Nails, other members of the Cadre were quietly referring men to us to talk about their various concerns.

Toward the end of March, both Howie and I were promoted to E-3, Privates First Class! We were gob smacked, given all the antiwar work we were doing. It turns out this bump in rank and small increase in pay was routine, based on time served in the military. In our minds, our promotion was still unbelievable. It was a welcome award (especially the marginally increased pay), but Howie and I and several others would soon be tested as angry clouds rumbled over the remaining men of the Bay of Pigs.

Thirty-Sixth

———•———

Orderly Room

> Pay special attention to those who,
> by the accidents of time, or place, or circumstances,
> are brought into closer connection with you.
>
> Augustine of Hippo

Each morning I would jump on Interstate 5 from our cabin in the woods and head to the base. On clear days, Mount Rainier dominated the background and beckoned to me from the east, easing my commute during this relatively mild, Seattle winter weather.

I settled into the job quickly. Given what I was used to in army life, being a clerk was remarkable, like working a normal job. We reported to the orderly room by about 0800 hours (8:00 AM) checking out about 1700 hours (5:00 PM), with an hour for lunch, usually at the mess hall. I'd hang out with my buddies from the Bay of Pigs at lunch and often for a time after work.

There was much typing to be done. The Army had forms for just about everything. This was relatively simple; but now and again I would be asked to transcribe the written notes from a troop seeking a reassignment or requesting some other action. These were often poorly written, and I suspected they were likely not to succeed. I talked to Sergeant Nails about it and he told me to take necessary action to improve the narratives. Let's just say I gratuitously exercised a little literary license, hoping to build a case for the guy that might be more effective.

———•———

A short time later, Nails called me over to his desk. He said he had been watching how I work and appreciated how I tried hard to help guys with their different issues. He said something like, "I know you and your conscientious objector buddies want to get discharged. I get it, you don't want to be here. Neither do the guys who come here desperate for reassignments or with other situations. From now on I want you to meet with some of these guys, truly understand their problems, and help them prepare their case; maybe it will help them get approval for their requests." I was shocked. Nails wanted me to counsel these guys, find solutions, and help them prepare their material! Imagine that, suddenly, I morphed from a coarse and common maggot to a twenty-one-year-old, shake-and-bake social worker. No one was more surprised than me.

I did not keep track of the number of guys I tried to help, but I did meet with several desperate men. I do not want to overstate this. Most of those who came to the orderly room were seeking mundane things like weekend passes or leaves for rest and recreation. Nails never sent those guys to me. But some troops wanted medical discharges, others sought hardship reassignments or asked to be sent to bases closer to home or to delay or prevent their transfer to another base or country.

Of course, my favorite cases were guys who came in with conscience qualms about the war or their role in the military. Some had gone to chaplains but were not satisfied with what they heard or what they were told to do. Generally, that advice had been to pray more, man up, and do their duty.

By this point I had done a fair amount of reading about military issues and had some experience under my belt. I'd heard some desperate stories before, but this was the first time I was able to make a contribution that just might have an impact in the lives of some of my peers.

I realized quickly what I needed to do was to shut up and listen; to let the guys get stuff off their minds and then give some thoughts on how they might proceed. Perhaps they would need to do more research, provide more documentation, or get in contact with GI-Civilian antiwar groups, JAG lawyers, or others who were out there to help.

———•———

For the most part, however, some poor guy would show up needing assistance with the everyday problems of living a military life. I recall being successful with a handful of cases that succeeded in getting men reassigned or having their orders changed. And yet, many decisions were often arbitrarily denied, which made us both very frustrated and angry.

My greatest challenge was working with a guy I'll call "Jake" who was on emergency leave from his second tour in Vietnam. Jake arrived looking anxious, haggard, tense, and worried.

This poor fellow had a wife with serious mental-health problems requiring his presence. I noticed he constantly fidgeted, his furled brow and sad eyes accentuating the obvious fatigue engulfing him.

Jake was no slacker; indeed, he was proud to admit being a helicopter door gunner in Nam. With some pride, and no little amount of snark, he reported he had shot up many people and things. This is what he did—and claimed he liked it. He had seen much action during his first tour and was all too often on the cutting edge of danger. After that tour, he came back to the states; but like many other combat veterans, he got antsy, craved the excitement of being in a war zone, and volunteered to be sent back.

Apparently, more than a year of concern and worry had put his fragile wife over the edge. Now he was back home again, a proven jungle fly-boy who was looking for some courtesy from an organization he had served so well. He had nothing left to prove; he just wanted to be reassigned to a U.S. base closer to his family home.

The first thing I did after hearing his story was to tell him I would be glad to help process his request, but he needed to know he was working with a guy who was opposed to the war. Perhaps I wasn't the right guy for the job; maybe he would be more comfortable working with a lifer or another in-country Vietnam veteran. He listened closely to my story and had no problem whatsoever working with me. He understood I was not anti-GI but antiwar and anti-militarism. Consider us the Odd Couple; both in solidarity and when it came to this issue, both on the same page.

Jake and I worked hard on his paperwork further documenting his wife's condition, his time in Vietnam, and writing a narrative suggesting he had gone above and beyond the normal call of duty. Therefore, we argued, his modest request for reassignment to the States should be approved.

Nails checked it out and sent it up the chain of command. A week or so later we were notified that his request had been denied. Worse, within days he was told to report to the Overseas Replacement Center to head back to Vietnam. I was frustrated and extremely annoyed. This whole thing pissed me off, even as Nails tried hard to calm me down. I felt this should have been a slam dunk. If anyone deserved compassionate treatment it was this guy.

Jake, too, was livid. This committed, young, potential military lifer had been abandoned by the very organization he professed to love. He now did not want anything to do with the U.S. Army, and said he preferred to get out. He told me we should now apply for a discharge. Otherwise, he would go AWOL.

Nails and I encouraged Jake to stand down, to go through the motions in preparation for shipment, while I tried to find another way to help him out. I was at wits end. I just did not have the juice to pull strings nor the experience needed to find a way around this. Then it struck me; if I was a civilian and needed some good information, I would call a librarian—they found answers to everything. But who would I call here? In this case I needed to talk to people on the base with similar access to information. Company clerks! The head company clerk seemed to know everything about policy and procedure and, along with his orderly room sergeants, usually was the one who got things done.

Our own company clerk was not sure anything could be done, but he suggested I call a couple of clerks in other units. I picked up the phone and started calling around. Finally, I got referred to a guy who was not only sympathetic but had some answers. He told me once a troop's reassignment request was denied he could not then ask for a discharge *at the same duty station*. He told me to get Jake's orders to report to the Fort Lewis Overseas Replacement Center rescinded and have them replaced with orders to ship from another base.

As I recall, Jake lived in California, so we lied to the brass asking them to cancel his orders and schedule him to ship from Presidio, a base in California. We argued that with a switch to California he could spend a few days dealing with critical family problems before shipping back to Vietnam, something he could not do from Fort Lewis.

Once we got approval, I told Jake to report to the Presidio and immediately present his paperwork and request a hardship discharge. Rumor had it Jake was in fact discharged, but I have to admit I do not know how Jake's story played out. I don't remember if a formal notice trickled back to us, and I never heard from him again. I would like to believe in this case the Army stepped up and took care of one of its own, but I was beyond being jaded and could only hope for the best.

This entire experience built my confidence and further emboldened me, and not a day too soon. Storm clouds were rising over the Bay of Pigs that would overtake several of us. I, for one, was ready for more action. So were many of the others; our time had come.

— • —

The letter from the Reverend Lieutenant Colonel K rejecting my claim of conscientious objection had been my first setback. His brief but powerful rejection was now attached to the package being sent up the chain of command at Fort Lewis and would eventually make its way to Washington, DC.

Also included were recommendations from my unit's Company Commander and the Attorney General (AG) of the Personnel Action Division. The interview I had with my Company Commander had also been less than satisfying. The young Lieutenant now in this position would soon be discharged from the army and had much to do before he left. It was clear he did not want to engage with me, as he was overwhelmed with the paperwork already on his desk. For the most part, this was a one-sided conversation with me stating my position and him concentrating on his piles of paper. Toward the end of the "interview," he admitted he had not read my application for discharge which he considered "shit." Of course, I did not arrive there with great expectations and surely did not leave feeling encouraged.

The interview with the AG was not overly confrontational. He was, after all, an attorney. The meeting started off pleasantly and the AG took some time to read through the application. When he was finished, he did not ask for any further clarifications nor did he attempt to rebut anything I had written. The AG did ask what he referred to as an "unfair question," which was, would I have applied as a conscientious objector if the present war was not in progress. I answered, without reservation, saying I did not consider the Cold War Era a time of peace. But beyond that, I considered my exposure to military life a learning period and as a result came to understand I was living in contrast to the dictates of both conscience and belief. I said even if I had entered the service during peacetime or given noncombatant status, I would have come to the same conclusion.

I left the meeting feeling like I had received a decent hearing. I appreciated his friendliness, but by this point I did not trust it. Nevertheless, I hoped his letter would be supportive. What I did not know was his report was not supportive at all; rather the AG wrote, "…his religious beliefs are not sufficient enough to warrant discharge…."

I was also not aware my request was subsequently disapproved at the command level and again by a Colonel at the Adjutant General's office. The former said, "…[the] application is based on personal moral code and philosophical views developed after entry into the service, which disqualifies him…." The Adjutant General agreed, writing, "…application is based on EM's [Enlisted Man's] personal moral code rather than by reason of religious training and belief….."

———•———

Again, at this point, I was only aware of the chaplain's submission. I had taken direct action as soon as I learned about it by sending copies to attorney Chas Talbot and to the Catholic Peace Fellowship who had been supportive and helpful. Shortly after my return to Fort Lewis in January 1969, their powerful and supportive response letters arrived.

Talbot fired back in a formidable missive to Reverend K, writing:

> I am struck by the conclusion of your letter that his basis for objection to service "is not a religious interpretation of the Catholic faith."
>
> I do not know how the reviewing authorities will be able to determine from your letter what you have

relied on in reaching this conclusion…and I therefore strongly request, nay insist, that your letter be supplemented by a letter that sets out in detail the basis of your conclusion.

Then, using a strong personal insight, he fired for effect saying:

One of the recurring problems I see…is an apparent unwillingness of chaplains and the Catholic faith to recognize and admit that a Roman Catholic can, consistent with the teachings of the Church, be a total conscientious objector.

The Catholic Peace Fellowship responded with two letters. Writing to me, they said:

I am very much impressed with the clarity and force of your expression. You have obviously given the matter of your own Christian responsibility…to war and peace long and prayerful consideration. We have seldom seen as clear a case as yours. You have the support of the Catholic Peace Fellowship in your demand for recognition of your rights as a sincere conscientious objector to war…and we pledge you any assistance we can.

Addressing Reverend K, a counselor wrote:

To be frank, Father, I am astounded that you are able to dismiss the claim of this young man so cavalierly. To assert that "the basis for his objection is not a religious interpretation of the Catholic faith" is gratuitous at best and to say the least uninformed.

…the Constitution on the Church in the Modern World calls explicitly for the recognition of the rights of conscientious objection to war. The U.S. Bishops Conference in its latest pronouncements has gone beyond this to call for the recognition of the rights of "selective" conscientious objection….

In this particular case, Father, the claim that Private Gioglio presents…is exceptionally strong…. We may not agree with every one of his formulations, but we can all see the depth of conviction and the steadfastness of faith that inform his conscience. I respectfully ask you to intercede for this young man so that his rights as a Christian and as an American citizen be protected…I cannot see how you can do otherwise.

Strong stuff. I was moved and gratified by their support. I was also shocked; never before had I witnessed a priest being challenged so vigorously. I sent the responses up the chain of command and it appears they were included in the package forwarded to the Department of Defense for final approval.

———•———

I now had full access to a typewriter at the orderly room, and decided the time had come to get more fully involved in peace work and to be more open about it. During lunch and slow times, I used the typewriter to advance my case. I also began typing letters to Congress and peace groups, and sending other missives. Within weeks, I joined the Catholic Peace Fellow-ship. Then, after some serious reflection and ongoing doubts, I joined the international organization, The War Resisters League, which required members to agree *all* war was a crime against humanity.

I also wrote to the St. Francis of Assisi Roman Catholic Church in Tacoma volunteering to speak on Catholicism and conscientious objection. I also sent a proposed article to the Fellowship of Reconciliation journal, the *Fellowship*. I do not remember being invited to speak at St. Francis, nor if the arti-cle was accepted. However, I was not discouraged; slowly, I was learning success did not necessarily mean achievement but rather engagement and striving for change.

These activities and plans did not go unnoticed. By the end of January 1969, the frequency of low-level harassment directed toward me and other Bay of Pigs residents increased. Several of us found ourselves being written up for non-judicial, Article 15 violations of the Uniform Code of Military Justice. These were low level violations of standard operating procedure said to require something more than an "oral admonition or repri-mand." Article 15-worthy punishments were often reported by members of the Military Police, sort of like parking tickets handed out by traffic cops. On occasion, MPs would show up in places where GIs gathered, like in the PX, looking for perceived, petty violations. A few times, two or more of us were written up at the same time. This led us to believe we were under obser-vation and being singled out for punishment. In reality, these Mickey Mouse tactics had little to do with our comportment or how we looked and more to do with being identified as consci-entious objectors.

In my case, I received three Article 15s by the end of January, one for "wearing a Kitchen Police cap," one because they said my "hair exceeded the prescribed length," and a third said my "moustache [also] exceeded the prescribed length."

The officer conducting my hearing decided the last two charges were actionable, but he dismissed the charge of wearing a floppy fatigue cap, since that was the only headgear I had ever been issued. At the time, the army was transitioning to olive-drab baseball caps, but not everyone had been issued the new headgear. I was lucky this time around, the hearing officer decided I would forfeit $10 pay that month from my basic allotment of $113 for my coiffure. Some of the others did not fare as well, forfeiting some pay for months or being assigned extra duties.

None of this petty harassment dissuaded us.

Thirty-Seventh

—•—

Sanctuary

Bad times, hard times, this is what people keep saying;
but let us live well, and times shall be good.
We are the times: Such as we are, such are the times.

Augustine of Hippo

I did find a sense of peace and respite at the Shelter Half Coffee House and, of course, at the little cabin we rented outside the base. The place was sparsely furnished but more than adequate. It was off the beaten path and surrounded by trees; a little piece of heaven on the outskirts of madness. There was no television. That was good because it allowed time for building my case and giving thought to other antiwar activities both on and off the base; bad, because that mindless avenue of escape was not conveniently at hand.

Connie, my wife at the time, had a part-time job, working I believe at a nursing home. The income from it helped keep our heads above the water financially, even if we did scratch around from time to time looking for loose change. Despite the economic distress, this cabin in the woods was in and of itself escape from the reality of the situation we confronted, even as I became constantly preoccupied, edgy, and less than available on many levels. Looking back, I see it must have been hard for my young wife. Still, she persevered and was always loyal and supportive.

Our neighbor in the cabin next-door was a disabled combat veteran. He and his wife were country kids, soft-spoken, and not well educated. Like many others, they could not wait to be discharged and head home. He had a shunt sticking out of his side, the result of a deep shrapnel wound suffered over there. A disillusioned survivor, he had been a gung-ho enlistee, but he had seen too much and no longer supported the war. We shared some stories and he was glad to hear of my decision to resist and my in-service involvement in the peace movement. His immediate wounded presence angered me and bolstered my resolve to resist the war and somehow help bring it to an end.

—■•■—

Now and again, I walked over to an open space by the nearby lake for a few moments of quiet reflection. Subconsciously, the memory of the peaceful time alone listening to music at the USO near Fort Polk and the remarkable moment of insight I experienced there one day beckoned me to sit quietly and simply engage in this way. Something I still do to this day.

All things considered I was not a deeply prayerful kid. Like many in my generation I had simply learned to pray an established set of prayers taught to us in religion class. I did not recall any reference to the idea of staying still, of listening for answers to one's prayers; no attention paid to the contemplative experience, or of doing anything other than rote petitioning prayer; only approaching the Divine like a child begging a parent, basically throwing needs out there and hoping for a good result. I never heard a word about contemplative prayer, nor was I aware of the plethora of Christian mystics who promoted that spiritual practice. I did not have connection to a spiritual advisor, two words I did not even know existed. Thus, for the most part, I continued to pray using the tools I had learned, but they did not give me much peace.

I did not realize being stuck this way spiritually was often counter-productive. I drifted a bit, looking for other escapes and answers, in the counterculture and in alcohol. Finally, almost by extension, I stumbled upon meditation. The counterculture's mantra to "Tune in, turn on, and drop out" appealed to many in those years, and it seemed like an attractive thing to do. Tune into the music and current thought. Turn on by using chemicals, drugs, or alcohol. Drop out of the dominant society, perhaps by joining a commune. The youth culture of our time seemed to be experimenting with new ways of being, but all too often our generation was unconsciously borrowing utopian thought from the past. For example, the ancient practice of Eastern meditation was being "rediscovered" and promoted.

Also, there were priests like Thomas Merton, a Trappist monk who was a powerful advocate for peace and forcefully voiced opposition to nuclear weapons. Unfortunately, I was only marginally aware of his position on these issues. Merton's ideas were in books and magazines I did not read, nor were his messages heard in any of the pulpits I experienced. In addition, I knew nothing of his writings on contemplation or his familiarity with Christian mysticism or Eastern spirituality. Nevertheless, in the muddled countercultural philosophy of the time, Merton's messages were apparently familiar to many, and I have read him since.

The renewed interest in Eastern philosophy and spirituality also manifested itself through the actions, behaviors, and teaching of Maharishi Mahesh Yogi. This modern guru popularized a form of what he called "transcendental meditation," a practice so intriguing it was picked up and promoted by the Beatles, one of the musical super groups of all time.

I was aware, albeit somewhat skeptical, about all this. My untrained exercises in following my breath, centering, and emptying the mind were always overpowered by all sorts of everyday concerns. There seemed to be too many things going on preventing me from meditating too deeply. For the neophyte spiritual seeker, the emptying of self seems impossible. Nevertheless, I tried meditation from time to time, both before and after induction into the army. Memories of the one amazing experience I had when I was in Advanced Infantry Training should have drawn me in further, but my spiritual immaturity, as well as time and circumstance, always seemed to keep me from regular practice. I remember a few occasions when I would slip into an empty chapel on base or head down to the lake to sit quietly. This was peaceful and relaxing, but rarely was I able to silence the thoughts running amok in my brain.

At the time, the psychedelic vibe was very prominent in the Seattle area, featuring the current music purposely designed to draw people in, and take them "up, up, and away" in ways only music can. One night, while listening to a local rock station, I got mesmerized by a melodic, spacy song. It drew me in as I let my cares, thoughts, and worries fall away. It was as if it was just me and the sound, all wrapped up together, all one thing; I just let go and went with it. And then it happened. Once again, I experienced a deep chill amid an inner peace that was both extraordinary and unexplainable. Overwhelmed, my eyes snapped open; feeling confused, yet hyper-alert, I knew, just knew, I would not be going to Vietnam.

I heard no voices, received no direction, but for the second time since being drafted I was awarded with another indelible impression I dared not question or overthink. I sat there, much like an excited toddler enchanted by the first few tastes of ice cream or a young man in the afterglow of his first sexual experience. It was a mixture of satisfaction, awe, diffidence, and trepidation. There I was—shocked, a bit scared, absolutely amazed, and even partially amused.

When my head cleared, once again I decided it was best not to delve too deeply into what these two mystical experiences, separated by months, were all about. I didn't have the skills to do it anyway. I just knew the first experience suggested I would not be going to prison and this second one indicated I would not be heading for Vietnam. Somehow, I recognized these two things to be absolutely true. But how can you know what seems to be so incongruent, unknowable, and unpredictable? And yet,

I knew what I knew, with the same assurance I had that resisting the war and working for peace were the right things to do.

Once again, I told nobody else about this. Not my wife; not the disgruntled, wounded vet in the cabin next door; not the guys from the Bay of Pigs; not my family; not even the other resisters I've met over the years. I guess I always wanted to talk to someone about these two experiences, but it seemed too unbelievable; who would understand? Consider the possible reactions: outright dismissal, a bored, glassy-eyed look, amused disbelief; concern about my mental health. Or, at best, perhaps coming from an old hippie, "Far out, Man!" It just seemed better to keep both events to myself. Besides, the insights were for me alone and somehow, I intuitively knew it was up to me to simply embrace them. I am sharing them with you only to give the complete story of what happened to me during those complicated and difficult days.

Thirty-Eighth

—•—

Fighting Back

Keep on adding, keep on walking, keep on progressing:
do not delay on the road, do not go back, do not deviate.

Augustine of Hippo

By the beginning of April 1969, Howie and I received notice the Department of Defense had rejected our requests for discharge. In my case they wrote, "The applicant's objection to service is based upon a personal moral code." This was a devastating, if not an all-too-predictable response. Of course, we were both deeply disappointed, but undaunted and far from being defeated.

I must admit I was having difficulty dealing with the constant emotional and spiritual struggle. Howie and I could now be issued orders to ship to Vietnam at any time. There were infrequent, but intense, moments of doubt and temptation: should I compromise with the army and accept a noncombatant position? Or, like our buddy Covington, should I leave the country by simply taking a short ride from Washington State to Canada?

But leaving America was still something I could not come to grips with. Beyond leaving home and family, the idea of not staying and struggling did not sit right with me. More than ever, leaving seemed like the wrong thing to do.

My struggle was mostly spiritual, but in the frailty of the human moment it was unrecognized as such. The thoughts of escape, along with the fear of the unknown, were always present, as was the struggle to fight them off. It was obvious I would soon be reaching a decision point. More and more, it appeared working within the system was impractical for those of us opposed to the war.

———•———

I continued to have jumbled up notions of what it meant to be patriotic, of right and wrong, and how to proceed and what to do. Much of this was inexperience mixed with the raw anger of a youth caught up in a war and a system designed to make willing participants out of the socialized, the powerless, and the doubtful.

But I got off the pity-pot and took comfort in the two remarkable experiences I had: I knew in my soul that I was not going to prison or to Vietnam. I knew I must soldier on, defend my position, and go on the offensive when it came to antiwar activities. I decided it was better to stand tall and continue to risk the repercussions that might lie ahead.

Things would change rapidly over the next few months. Attorney Chas Talbot leapt into action. He immediately had

Howie and me file a second application for discharge as conscientious objectors. This would supplement the original application by clarifying how our beliefs had crystallized further. The reprieve also allowed us to be more involved in antiwar activity. We filed our applications and buckled our seatbelts, hoping for a better response.

In early May, Talbot suggested the two of us take the Fort Lewis authorities to Federal court. The idea was to file a habeas corpus complaint against the U.S. Army for "arbitrarily and capriciously" denying our applications for discharge. In the process, we might set a precedent for other conscientious objectors whose applications for discharge were routinely being denied. The court filing would assert those denied discharge under these grounds were essentially being held against their will and should be released from the military.

It sure sounded good to us. We would not only be helping ourselves, but if the habeas corpus action was granted it would permit the Federal court to intervene in military affairs, essentially changing the way conscientious objector applications were adjudicated. Howie and I signed on knowing full well we did not have the financial wherewithal to cover additional legal costs. Then again, we knew Chas was onto something very important that might help many others who were conscientiously opposed to the war.

The guys in the Bay of Pigs were very excited about this and offered much advice. One thought we should go public and seek financial support. One suggested we place an advertisement in the *New Republic* magazine, which was known for open-mindedness in politics and American life. The ad appeared a couple of times in early May 1969. It included a return mail address and read: "2 GIs Conscientious Objectors (Catholic, Buddhist) disapproved 'personal moral code.' Wish to set precedents. Habeas corpus. Need money."

We expected hate mail and perhaps a few donors. We only got one reply, a supportive note from a woman wishing us best and including a dollar. The fundraiser was an utter failure, but we considered this a moral victory as the antiwar ad was probably seen by many readers of the magazine.

———•———

The case was heard on May 27 in the Seattle courtroom of a federal judge. I had never been in a civilian courtroom before. I remember this one to be large, wood-lined, and imposing. It was certainly far more formal and daunting than the slapdash settings thrown together for the military court martials I attended. The no-nonsense judge seemed ancient to me, stately, somewhat perturbed, and clearly aware of the power he brandished.

When called to order, the officer from the Judge Advocate General's office simply asked the court to dismiss the habeas corpus motion insisting the military should adjudicate its own legal issues.

Chas argued, in our case, that the army had refused to accept Buddhism as a religion or recognize legitimate antiwar teachings in Catholicism. He proclaimed this narrow and subjective interpretation was both widespread and uninformed. This made it difficult for soldiers to be heard fairly or obtain discharges based on conscientious objection. His arguments were eloquent, thoughtful, and precise. I remember sitting there believing deeply in the American judicial system and in what I considered to be the strength of our case.

The proceedings took less than ten minutes. The judge quickly sided with the army and dismissed the habeas corpus action. Chas was flustered, if not downright angry. We were disappointed, once again battered but not broken. We knew this resistance from inside the military needed to be done and it was worth it. The Associated Press picked up the story and sent it out to their network of newspapers. Within a couple days, the *Seattle Daily Times* and the *Portland Oregonian* printed articles on the case. One read, "Judge Denies Plea of GIs," the other, "Soldiers Suit Thrown Out." Once again, the message that GIs were standing up to the Vietnam War and fighting back from inside the army hit the papers. Another important moral victory.

———•———

I continued to perform Orderly Room duties while my second application for discharge made its way up the chain. Meanwhile, guys periodically showed up seeking help with various problems. I kept trying to help them get relevant information while offering some suggestions on moving forward. The guys and I continued to hang out at the Shelter Half; we would pick up literature and some of us surreptitiously kept distributing fliers and newspapers around the base.

One night when a few of us were at the Shelter Half, a couple of University of Washington students sat down at our table and joined the conversation. They claimed they lived nearby and invited us to come back to their apartment for a couple beers and to meet up with other antiwar friends. We looked at each other, nodded agreement, and decided to go. Why not?

Free beer, a laidback atmosphere, good company. We jumped into the car and followed them to their place.

The living room was sparsely decorated with a comfortable looking couch and chairs. But our eyes were drawn to a bright red banner with a gold hammer and sickle hanging over the couch. Our hosts were Communists and apparently were trying to recruit us. We knew very little about Marxism; I knew virtually nothing about Stalinism, Maoism, Trotskyism, or the differences among these persuasions. At that time in our young lives, we were not ready to listen to alternative political perspectives.

We looked at each other with mutual concern. We were Americans placing our trust in our democracy. As kids, we had been deeply socialized, taught to distrust and fear the "Reds." We all lived through the Cuban nuclear incident where the U.S. and Russia came close to turning both countries into smoke and rubble. We had all been told Russia was our enemy and a creeping Communism, known as "the domino theory," was making its way around the world. According to the government, our guys were sent to Korea and Vietnam to keep those particular dominos from falling. Of course, we all rejected the story, even as we understood the North Vietnamese and the Vietcong were receiving weapons from Communist nations that they used against our guys. But as much as we hated this, it was out of our control. Nevertheless, as Americans, we could still actively oppose this never-ending conflict by forcing our government to listen to the soldiers and civilians who were opposed to the war.

In those days, antiwar activists were frequently called "Reds" or "commies." That is, if you were opposed to the war, you must be, or must have been, influenced by the Communists. Many of us heard things like, "This is not peace, this is Communism," or "If you don't like it here, move to Russia." But we were fighting to change the American system from within and none of us saw a need for assistance from other political or economic philosophies.

Being around our "hosts" did not sit well with any of us and we did not want to hear anything they had to say. With nods of agreement, we mumbled thanks but no thanks, turned around and left. Disillusioned and introspective, we jumped into the car for an unusually quiet ride back to the base.

———•———

One day while typing away at the Orderly Room, I decided to take a new antiwar action. I had a feeling I was running out of time and felt the pressure of possibly leaving Fort Lewis, by choice or by fiat. I was still flustered by the tepid response of the clergy on base and got the idea to write to the chaplains at Fort Lewis urging them to take a strong moral position against the war. I came up with a list of about a dozen members of the clergy, typed the letters, and signed each individually, making sure I used my new rank. These letters from Pfc. Gioglio soon got the brass' attention.

Sergeant Nails had no choice but to get me out of the office, much to his chagrin at losing a typist and ersatz counselor. I was immediately sent to the Repair and Utilization (R&U) room to do details like painting, cutting grass, and maintaining equipment. I heard, but cannot confirm, that one of the chaplains had actually spoken out against the war. I was also told this Rabbi was quickly assigned to another duty station, allegedly in Utah. All things considered, I felt pretty good about taking that action, although I must admit I was not too happy about losing regular access to a typewriter and telephone.

There was only one other guy working at R&U, a lowly Sargent E-5, recently out of the stockade. He had been busted in rank and was just putting in time waiting for discharge. Blackie was a severely alienated Nam combat vet who was fed up with military life and could not wait to get out of there. He cared little about the work needing to be done and found all sorts of ways to slow things down or grind them to a halt. Blackie said he spent time in the stockade after going AWOL and disappearing in the California desert. He no longer supported the war and after we exchanged stories, he encouraged me to keep resisting and trying to help other guys.

Blackie said he was happy to look the other way if I wanted to move some of the counselling and antiwar work to R&U. He just did not want me to bring in underground newspapers or fliers for fear of being accused of distributing literature; this was not a problem as our guys knew better than to store contraband in places where they might be discovered.

My Bay of Pigs mates and I were thrilled. We continued to help others who would trickle in looking for help. Regardless of the problems these troops confronted, we considered them all to be potential resisters or conscientious objectors; and now we had a place on base, outside the Bay of Pigs, where we could meet, talk, and plan actions.

In the meantime, none of our guys had been discharged for conscientious objection, but we soon lost another member of our group. One day, Jeff's application for discharge was disapproved by the Department of Defense. He was issued orders to report to the Overseas Replacement Center for shipment to Vietnam. True to form, he respectfully declined, and was charged with disobeying orders. Jeff was sent to the stockade to await a general court martial. While there, he found some support by hooking up with a few other incarcerated conscientious objectors and other resisters. They continued their antiwar work while there, telling their stories and encouraging people not to ship to Vietnam once they left the stockade.

—•—

Jeff was tried in another makeshift courtroom. It was another nondescript meeting room of some sort. A few collapsible lunch tables served as desks for the officers who would decide his future. Jeff, his lawyer, and the prosecuting attorney also sat at tables facing the judges. His young wife and those of us given permission to attend sat in support and anticipation on the folding chairs set out for the audience.

Once again, the issue was decided on extremely narrow grounds; that is, whether he disobeyed an order from a superior officer. This time, the judges did allow his civilian attorney to speak about the war, but it made little difference. The prosecution asked Jeff only one question, whether he disobeyed an order from his company commander. Which, of course, he did.

The officers deliberated for only a few minutes. Jeff was sentenced to three years of hard labor with a dishonorable discharge. Some of us stood silently as Jeff was escorted out of the courtroom and returned to the stockade for transmittal to Fort Leavenworth prison. Once again, we were angry and brokenhearted. But we were proud of him and strengthened by his witness. Jeff was just one more veteran who was a casualty of the war-against-the-war.

In late May, all the conscientious objectors associated with the Bay of Pigs were notified we were restricted to base for the Memorial Day holiday weekend. Allegedly, we were part of the skeleton crew ordered to keep the base operational during the four-day break. In reality, this was simply a shot over the bow: small-minded payback for our ever-increasing activism. None of us were assigned anything important; but rather we roamed around the perimeter of the base policing the grounds by picking up trash and cigarette butts.

On July 13, the civilians from the GI-Civilian Alliance for Peace staged what they called an "Aquatic Invasion of Fort Lewis." It was an act of guerrilla theater said to be conducted to "liberate the GIs on our base." A handful of rowboats paddled over from the civilian side of American Lake with some civilians dressed in fatigues.

Of course, they were immediately detained by the Military Police and held for a bit before being released. The press covered this theater of the absurd and the story was widely distributed. None of the guys at the Bay of Pigs had anything to do with this, but we did get a good laugh from it. It was inspiring to know the linkages between GIs and civilians had strengthened.

———•———

Little did I know I was coming to the end of this journey. A day or so after the Aquatic Invasion, Howie and I were told to "get over to the orderly room NOW, the CO wants to see you!" We knew being summoned to the Commanding Officer was not good. Did he want to question us about possible involvement in the protest? Had we once again been busted for some sort of mild transgression? Had our most recent applications for C.O. discharges been rejected? Was he about to order us to Vietnam? Were we about to join Rudy and Jeff at Ft. Leavenworth prison? Expecting the worst, we were absolutely astounded to hear our requests for discharge had been approved by the Department of Defense. Remarkably, we would both be honorably discharged in a couple days. We were told to go for one final medical exam, pack up our gear, and be ready to get out. We were overjoyed. I was stunned; shaken to my core.

How did this happen? Why were we discharged and not imprisoned? At some point, I used the Freedom of Information Act to request military and civilian intelligence files to try to find out. While this material did not answer those questions, the documents provided important details used in this book. For example, I did learn we had been under observation. There were also military intelligence witness statements from two officers and three members of the Cadre who were all sergeants. The officers said I had a "high degree of consciousness (or feeling) against the war." However, they also called me a "coward" and neither considered me a loyal American.

On the other hand, the three Noncommissioned Officers I worked with had a different view. All suggested a "high degree of moral character" stemmed from my religious beliefs and all considered me a loyal American. These differing perspectives are just another example of the enduring class differences between officers and those in the lower ranks.

More to the point, the military services were beginning to discharge many more conscientious objectors from their ranks. As the number of applications rose, so did the number of discharges, rising from 28% of the applications in 1967 and increasing steadily to 77% in 1972 (Cortright, p. 16-17). This suggests to me that the focus was on purging the ranks of the most vocal and active conscientious objectors. The exact reason they made this decision, however, remains a mystery to me.

Thirty-Ninth

———— ❖ ————

Mama Said There'd Be Days Like This

The journey is essential to the dream.

Francis of Assisi

Our telephone conversation went very much like this:
"Hi, Mom, it's Jerry."

Expressions of worry and concern.

"Slow down, no bad news today. Mom. Everything's fine. I called with some very good news, and I have to ask you for a favor. Earlier today I was told the discharge I requested has been approved. I'll be coming home soon."

Expressions of surprise and confusion.

"No, no, it is not a dishonorable or a bad conduct discharge. It's actually an honorable discharge on the basis of conscientious objection; there are no fines; I didn't violate any orders, so I won't be court martialed or sent to jail."

Sighs of relief and concern about future employment.

"Right, it won't affect my employment status in any way. Remember my old employer is holding my night job at the restaurant, so I'll be heading back there as soon as I get home."

More expressions of interest.

"Well, no, I won't be getting out today. Another guy and I are being discharged at the same time. We must take exit physicals and fill out some paperwork at a couple places. But I expect I'll be getting out of here in a couple days. Listen, if you can, I need your help. There are some bills to deal with, and I'm thinking about getting another vehicle, driving down the Pacific Coast, and seeing a bit of America before coming back East."

Anxious requests for more details and a promise to send some money.

"Yeah, you can stop worrying Mom. Everything's okay. It's unbelievable, but it really did happen and I'm very happy."

And then, in a voice that sparkled with a combination of disbelief, gratitude and humility, she simply said, "Oh, Jerry. Thank God."

Fortieth

———•———

Over and Out

> I have fought the good fight,
> I have finished the race.

2 Timothy 4:7

O n the morning of July 17, 1969, one year and fourteen days after being drafted, I was sent to a large open field swarming with other troops about to be discharged. Lines of GIs were backed up way beyond any other hurry-up-and-wait queue I'd ever experienced in the army. All of us about to be discharged; a herd of giddy, antsy, and somewhat apprehensive young men anxious to get back home.

———•———

An unrepentant maggot, such as myself, expected to be jerked around and at minimum sent to the back of the line. Surveying this mass of people, I figured I would be there all day, if not into the early evening. Remarkably, the sergeant in charge who checked me in, flashed me a dirty look, and simply barked, "Come with me, Private!" Much to my astonishment he escorted me to the head of the queue.

A couple of harried Spec-4s sat there among stacks of 201-personnel files and various other documents. A clerk checked the reason listed for my discharge and slammed down my file. He looked up in annoyance and disbelief and said to me, "You know, if you accept a discharge on the basis of conscientious objection you can never again enlist in this man's army or in any other branch of the military service." Then, more formally, he repeated similar words from a document requiring my verbal response. It read, "I fully understand that I am not eligible for voluntary enlistment in the army or in any other branch of the armed forces."

With an amazing amount of restraint, trying to mask great relief and joy, I baited him with, "Your kidding…. Well…okay then." He signed off on something and snapped the file into my chest. I was now a civilian, not a combat veteran but, inconceivably, an antiwar veteran; just another disillusioned young adult in 1969 America and, like everybody else being discharged, I was totally unprepared for what was to come. I grabbed my gear and left Fort Lewis.

—•—

A few days later I drove back to the base to say goodbye to Richard and Tom, the remaining members of our clique, and to some other guys at the Bay of Pigs. Packed and ready to go, I drove off, leaving the United States Army, but not its training, not its experience, and certainly not its war, behind.

THE END

Epilogue

Every moment and every event of every man's life on earth
plants something in his soul.

Rev. Thomas Merton, OCSO

Here is what happened to my fellow resisters from the Bay
of Pigs:

- Upon official review, Rudy's incarceration was reduced
  to twelve months and the dishonorable discharge was
  "upgraded" to a bad-conduct discharge. He was freed
  from prison after nine and a half months. Rudy did not
  let this experience disrupt his plans; he followed his
  dream and became a medical doctor.
- In addition to his time in the stockade, Jeff spent a total of
  fifteen months at Fort Leavenworth, released just before
  his twenty-second birthday.
- Tom was in and out of the Fort Lewis stockade. His second application for discharge was eventually accepted
  and he, like me, was honorably discharged for reasons of
  conscientious objection.

- Howie, also honorably discharged as a conscientious objector, followed his dreams and became a successful photographer.
- Richard spent the most time of all of us at the Bay of Pigs. He continually fought attempts to transfer him to another unit and happily did not spend any time in the stockade. By the time his second application for a conscientious objector discharge was disapproved, he only had about nine months left on his enlistment. Still, he fought on. About four months before his formal release date, he once again requested discharge on the basis of conscientious objection. That request was under review when his enlistment ended. Sometime later, he was notified he had indeed been honorably discharged as a conscientious objector.
- I lost track of AJ, the somewhat distant member of our circle. I also do not have information on how the remaining members of our dorm fared or how many future resisters came to call the Bay of Pigs their home.

———•———

In my case, it had been an intense twelve months of struggle and I was permanently changed. I was now an infantry soldier, a trained killer, a shake-and-bake counselor, a fledgling activist, and a very, very different young man. A classic contradiction wrapped inside a conundrum: the soldier who refused to kill; the veteran discharged as a conscientious objector; the conscientious objector who struggled with nonviolence; the spiritual neophyte who sought to navigate an ancient and beloved religion. There would be many more paradoxes to come. For years, as Richard might put it, I was "on the outside, inside."

In December 1969, the Shelter Half Coffeehouse in Seattle was designated "off limits" for all members of the military. However, it continued to serve the GI-civilian antiwar community until closing in 1974.

The My Lai massacre of unarmed civilians by U.S. troops became public knowledge in November 1969. The actual event occurred in March 1968 but had been kept under wraps during the entire time I was in the army. The announcement further galvanized opposition to the war among both the public and in the military. I could not help but flashback to the training we received and the effect it might have had on those troops who took out their frustration and anger on innocent civilians.

The Selective Service draft changed to a lottery system in late 1969. This meant young males were no longer universally subjected to the Selective Service process. Now, some men would potentially be called-up based on a random number chosen for their birthday. The date drawn determined the order of induction; that is, guys with lower numbers were more likely to be called for physicals and possibly drafted. All men were still required to register at age eighteen. However, this registration was suspended in 1976, effectively ending the draft. Universal registration for males only was once again mandated in 1980, but to date no more men have been conscripted. The Armed Forces continues to enlist only male and female volunteers—even if some choose military jobs solely due to economic conditions and the inability to afford college. In the minds of many, this is known as a "poverty draft."

In June 1971, the *New York Times* revealed the existence of the Pentagon Papers, publishing top-secret documents provided by Daniel Ellsberg, a military analyst who worked for the RAND Corporation. The Justice Department tried to stop further publication but failed. Soon the entire nation learned damning information about the war that contradicted ongoing government narratives and exposed secret operations such as the expansion of the Vietnam conflict into Cambodia and Laos.

After discharge, I became deeply engaged in the peace movement both as a community and student activist. I went back to college to study the social and geopolitical reasons for our country's involvement in Southeast Asia in an attempt to understand how we were all so easily sucked into this vortex. Despite shelves of books in my library and a lifetime of thought, I still cannot completely understand it.

One of the more insightful books, *In Retrospect: The Tragedy and Lessons of Vietnam* was written by Robert S. McNamara, a key proponent of the Vietnam War, the Secretary of Defense during both the Kennedy and Johnson Administrations. Here, McNamara admits he and other Administration officials made many mistakes in judgment and policy, knew the war was unwinnable, and suggested the United States should have withdrawn as early as 1963. Still, the government continued to promote the war, all the while failing to tell the truth about its futility. And so, the war raged on until 1975, leading to over 58,000 American and perhaps up to two million Southeast Asian deaths.

———•———

Shortly after discharge, I was trained as a draft counselor by my advocates at the Catholic Peace Fellowship. By then, more than ever I was convinced the war was illegal and conducted immorally. I knew young men continued to need help to secure their rights under the Selective Service System. I also believed the draft was something akin to involuntary servitude and guys who did not want to be in the military should not be inducted to fight wars of aggression against other nations. Nor, I believe, should they be made to serve alongside those who believe in a military life and in what they volunteered to do.

There were years of leafleting, antiwar organizing, letter writing, and visiting Congresspeople. Some of us refused to pay a telephone tax levied on American households to help fund the war. Locally, we opened a Peace Center. Nationally, we held frequent mass demonstrations, each with its own threatening combination of police dogs, horses, and armed men on rooftops standing against us. We walked carrying banners, unarmed and mostly unafraid. We sang and screamed "Peace Now!" even as we navigated urban mine fields, some of us constantly surveying the rooftops, the march participants, and the surrounding area—knowing at any moment it could all explode into confrontation and violence as it sometimes did, especially at Kent State University on May 4, 1970. For years, antiwar vets like Vietnam Veterans Against the War demonstrated and sponsored political theater prodding the government and civilians to do more to end the madness that was Vietnam. As veterans we marched, chanted, called antiwar cadence, flew banners, and carried the American flag. For a time, it seemed like the struggle for peace would never end. I guess it never really has.

For me, there followed years of dabbling in community organizing, student activism, and eventually union activity and leadership. I stood "with the people," becoming more and more progressive and political.

I did not believe I had changed, even though I often heard that I had from the people closest to me. I guess I was living with something of a melancholy disposition and a military mind that had been imbedded in me. Even today, doing things automatically, like practicing "Do. Don't think," sometimes results in less than positive outcomes for me.

I became more distrustful of government, secular authority, and for many years religious systems. I struggled to live a nonviolent life, but it was one periodically marked by outbursts of red-hot anger. It took decades to realize that to build a more peaceful world, you first have to build a more peaceful self. Then there was an ever-present need for escape through behaviors far beyond being out of character, far away from connecting with my better angel.

I suspect soldiers who complete Basic or Advanced Infantry Training but have no combat experience suffer some form of adjustment problems after leaving the military. Over the years I met many former members of the Bay of Pigs barracks at Fort Lewis and other resisters who reported various adjustment difficulties. It seems that adjustment to civilian life can be slow for many who experience *any form* of military exposure, including those who oppose or are incarcerated for refusing to participate in a war.

I suggest most young adults are not fully formed emotionally to handle the constant state of trauma experienced during basic and advanced combat trainings, and that the relentless effect of one traumatic thing after another amplifies over time. Warriors or not, we were all in the military and, depending on experience, too many of us endured emotional and moral damage, leaving indelible imprints on the soul.

Speaking as one resister, let me suggest that as antiwar soldiers we totally underestimated what it took to stand up to the full force of governmental and military power. No one is trained to do this. Doing so takes its toll; it takes something out of you. But just to be clear: I sure do not want to equate what those of us who encountered the war experience as trainees with the horrible combat experiences and subsequent adjustment problems confronted by the soldiers who have been sent to various war zones around the world.

—•—

Thirty years after my discharge, I watched *The Truce*, a Holocaust film based on a memoir written by Primo Levi in 1963. John Turturro was cast as Levi, an Italian-Jew living in Fascist Italy during World War II. Removed from his comfortable middle-class home, Levi was sent to an Italian concentration camp and eventually to Auschwitz in 1944.

Levi's book and the film teach important lessons to remember. He speaks of people's inhumanity toward others, how easily the peace and serenity of a dignified nation can be shattered by demagogues with militaristic or racist ideology, and how easily an entire population can be manipulated. Through sheer willpower and personal faith, Levi survived under extreme conditions until the camp was liberated in 1945.

In the film's last scene, we see Turturro, as the now-freed Primo Levi, sitting at a table in the library of his well-appointed home. He sits there preparing to write his memoirs, evoking memories of his ordeal. Before he begins, he unwraps a package containing his prison shirt from Auschwitz. The actor's sad and distant eyes project the sights and sounds being replayed in Levi's mind and troubled soul.

Why? Why would he hold on to such a thing—a threadbare reminder of a past that brought him so much pain? Was it some sort of inanimate muse that helped him write the unexplainable—a tangible piece of a disturbing past that must be kept forever? Was it a bell of mindfulness drawing him back to the pain, even as it allowed him to be grateful for the present moment he now inhabited? And yet, I know I am not alone among Vietnam veterans in doing something similar, like keeping watches set on 24-hour military time and wearing olive-drab Army-Navy surplus fatigue shirts—just because.

—•—

But let's not end this book's journey with such an undercurrent of melancholy and nostalgia. When antiwar GIs arrived on the scene, we blew the roof off the place. This was something new; it was not just individual opposition to an unpopular war, it was confrontation. It was guys in combat refusing to cooperate. Guys returning from Southeast Asia were taking a public stand against the war. Guys in training were refusing to ship to war zones. Guys stateside were going to prison or waging the in-service resistance.

At first neither the military nor civilians knew how to handle it. Eventually the military decided to clean house getting rid of "troublemakers" such as us conscientious objectors and then taking even greater control by instituting the all-volunteer armed forces we have today.

Soon after filing my conscientious objector claim, my Commanding Officer demanded to know what I would say to my children when they asked me, "What did you do in the war, Dad?"

With apologies for the fifty-year delay, this book is my humble response... Sir!

References

Books

Augustine of Hippo. (2003). *The Confessions.* Revised & Updated by Dr. Tom Gill. Translation by Albert C. Outler. Gainsville: Bridge-Logos.

Cortright, D. (1975). *Soldiers in Revolt: The American Military Today.* Garden City: Anchor Press/Doubleday.

Del Duca, R (2019). *Breaking Cadence: One Woman's War Against the War.* Portland: Ooligan Press.

Griffin, J. H. (1961). *Black Like Me.* Boston: Houghton Mifflin Company.

Gioglio, G. (1989). *Days of Decision: An Oral History of Conscientious Objectors in the Military During the Vietnam War.* Trenton: Broken Rifle Press.

Hartsouch, D., with Hollyday, J. (2014). *Waging Peace: Global Adventures of a Lifelong Activist.* Oakland: PM Press.

Jacobs, C. and Gallagher, J. (1967). *The Selective Service Act: A Case Study of Governmental Process.* New York: Dodd Mead & Company.

Kovic, R. (1976). *Born on the Fourth of July: A True Story of Innocence Lost and Courage Found.* New York: McGraw Hill.

Lembcke, J. (1998). *The Spitting Image: Myth, Memory, and the Legacy of Vietnam.* New York: New York University Press.

McNamara, R. (1995). *In Retrospect: The Tragedy and Lessons of Vietnam.* New York: Random House, Inc.

Mann, M. (2007). *To Benning & Back, Volume 1: The Making of a Citizen Soldier.* Indiana: Author House.

Marshall, S.L.A. (1947). *Men Against Fire: The Problem of Battle Command in Future Wars.* Alexandria, VA: Byrd Enterprises, Inc.

Morton, J. (2004). *Reluctant Lieutenant: From Basic to OCS in the Sixties.* College Station: Texas A&M University Press.

Moser, R. (1995). *The New Winter Soldiers: GI and Veteran Dissent During the Vietnam Era.* New Brunswick, NJ: Rutgers University Press.

Parsons, D. (2010). *Dangerous Grounds: Antiwar Coffeehouses and Military Dissent in the Vietnam Era.* Chapel Hill: University of North Carolina Press.

Perone, J. (2001). *Songs of the Vietnam Conflict.* Westport, Connecticut: Greenwood Press.

Simon, P. and Garfunkel, A. (1966). *The Sounds of Silence.* Columbia Records.

Springsteen, B. (2016). *Born to Run.* New York: Simon & Schuster.

Wittels, M. (1970*) Advice for Conscientious Objectors in the Armed Forces.* Philadelphia, PA: Central Committee for Conscientious Objectors.

Films

Warner Bros. (1987). *Full Metal Jacket.* Directed by Stanley Kubrick.

Tristar Pictures (1987). *Gardens of Stone.* Directed by Francis Ford Coppola.

Miramax Films. (1998). *The Truce.* Directed by Francesco Rosi.

ADVANCE PRAISE FOR
MARCHING TO A SILENT TUNE

Marching to a Silent Tune is a beautifully written, evocative, and frightening memoir of one dissenter's experiences in the environment of ubiquitous Vietnam-era militarism, with strong undercurrents of the absurdity with which the military of the time sought to fulfill its deadly "duty." Gerald Gioglio's heartfelt rejection of the military's machinations is both an historical overview of those turbulent times and a thought-provoking guidebook for young people contemplating entering the military today.

> —John Ketwig, Vietnam War veteran and author,
> *Vietnam Reconsidered: The War, the Times, and Why They Matter*

In these challenging times, ignorance is our greatest enemy. We need people like Jerry Gioglio who can give us wisdom and hope. In *Marching to a Silent Tune,* he does just that.

> —Roy Bourgeois, Vietnam War veteran, Catholic priest,
> and co-author, *My Journey from Silence to Solidarity*

I wasn't a conscientious objector, but I served with good men who were. It made me a better leader and our company a better band of brothers. It takes courage, conviction, and commitment to do what you believe is right, and getting bureaucracies like the U.S. Army to bend is not easy—anytime or in any generation.

> —Tom Mosgaller, Sergeant, U.S. Army, 1969-1972 and co-compiler,
> *Bending Granite: 30+ True Stories of Leading Change*

Every high school student, male and female, should read this book. Their parents should too.

> —Tom Cornell, Catholic Peace Fellowship and co-editor,
> *A Penny a Copy: Readings from the Catholic Worker.*